A POLITICAL HISTORY OF
POSTWAR ITALY

MODERN ITALY

A POLITICAL HISTORY OF
POSTWAR ITALY

From the Old to the New Center-Left

Norman Kogan

PRAEGER SPECIAL STUDIES • PRAEGER SCIENTIFIC

Library of Congress Cataloging in Publication Data

Kogan, Norman.
  A political history of postwar Italy.

  Bibliography: p.
  1. Italy—Politics and government—1945-1976.
2. Italy—Politics and government—1976-
3. Italy—Economic conditions—1945-1976. 4. Italy—
Economic conditions—1976-   . I. Title.
DG577.5.K63   945.092   80-28106
ISBN 0-03-056653-3

Published in 1981 by Praeger Publishers
CBS Educational and Professional Publishing
A Division of CBS, Inc.
521 Fifth Avenue, New York, New York 10175 U.S.A.

Printed in the United States of America

to
Richard, Frank, and Nan

PREFACE

In 1965 I wrote the book *A Political History of Postwar Italy* at the suggestion and with the encouragement of Frederick A. Praeger. The book covered the period from the Second World War to 1965. Having decided in 1978 that a sequel to that book would be appropriate, I worked on the present volume during 1979 and the first half of 1980. This volume carries forward the story of Italy from 1965 to today. As in the earlier book my chief concern here has been to narrate the principal developments of the last fifteen years. Since my interests are political and economic, these types of issues receive my primary attention. The period covered is so recent that by the nature of the case I cannot benefit from historical perspective. Nor have I had access to the primary documents that will become available only decades later. The book is written, therefore, from the public record: secondary sources, newspapers, and conversations with participants and observers. For this reason there are few footnotes, though I try to compensate for their scarcity with a longer bibliography.

I am grateful to many people for ideas, suggestions, encouragement. Over the years, The University of Connecticut has granted me the sabbatical leaves and other research support necessary for this and my earlier work. Dean Julius Elias of The University of Connecticut and Dean Hugh Clark of The University of Connecticut Research Foundation have been particularly generous with their personal and creative support. I owe a unique debt of gratitude to the Commission for Cultural Exchange between Italy and the United States and to its director, Dr. Cipriana Scelba. Professor Alberto Spreafico of the Italian Social Sciences Council and Professor Cesare Merlini of the Institute for International Affairs generously made their facilities available to me. At the University of Rome Professors Emilia Morelli and Carlo Mongardini extended every kindness to me. The Rockefeller Foundation provided me with a glorious month to work as a scholar in residence at its Bellagio Study and Conference Center on Lake Como.

My wife, Meryl, got me through this travail, providing me with all of her literary and moral support. She never permitted me to indulge in bouts of pessimism, either about this manuscript or about Italy. Both that country and I are fortunate to have such a fan. Betty

G. Seaver edited and typed this manuscript magnificently and did an even greater job of deciphering my handwriting.

The Italian people remain a marvelous enigma. After more than 35 years of paying attention, I am certain that I still do not understand them. But they are a key attraction drawing me back to that fascinating peninsula. My lack of understanding cannot excuse, however, any mistakes of fact or interpretation, for which I continue to take sole responsibility.

Norman Kogan
Storrs, Connecticut

CONTENTS

LIST OF TABLES

GLOSSARY

Political Parties

CPSU	Communist Party of the Soviet Union
DC	Democrazia Cristiana / Christian Democracy
DP	Democrazia Proleteria / Proletarian Democracy
MSI	Movimento Sociale Italiano / Italian Social Movement
MSI-DN	Movimento Sociale Italiano-Destra Nazionale / Italian Social Movement-National Right
PCF	Parti Communist Français / French Communist Party
PCI	Partito Communista Italiano / Italian Communist Party
PDIUM	Partito Democratico Italiano di Unità Monarchica / Italian Democratic Party of Monarchist Unity
PDUP	Partito Democratico di Unità Proletaria / Democratic Party of Proletarian Unity
PLI	Partito Liberale Italiano / Italian Liberal Party
PR	Partito Radicale / Radical Party
PRI	Partito Repubblicano Italiano / Italian Republican Party
PSDI	Partito Social Democratico Italiano / Italian Social Democratic Party
PSI	Partito Socialista Italiano / Italian Socialist Party
PSIUP	Partito Socialista Italiano di Unità Proletaria / Italian Socialist Party of Proletarian Unity

| PSU | Partito Socialista Unificato / Unified Socialist Party |
| SVP | Sud Tyroler Volkspartei / South Tyrol People's Party |

International and Regional Organizations

CAP	Common Agricultural Program
EEC	European Economic Community
GATT	General Agreement on Tariffs and Trade
IMF	International Monetary Fund
NATO	North Atlantic Treaty Organization
OECD	Organization for Economic Cooperation and Development
OPEC	Organization of Petroleum Exporting Countries

Finance and Tax Terms

IGE	Imposta Generale sul Esercizio / General Multiple Step Sales Tax
IVA	Imposta sul Valore Aggiunto / Value Added Tax
SDR	Special Drawing Rights

Trade Unions, Workers Organizations, and Trade Associations

ACLI	Associazione Cristiana di Lavoratori Italiani / Christian Association of Italian Workers
CGIL	Confederazione Generale Italiana di Lavoro / Italian General Confederation of Labor
CISL	Confederazione Italiana di Sindacati Lavoratori / Italian Confederation of Workers' Unions
Confindustria	Confederation of Industries (Private Sector)
ECFTU	European Confederation of Free Trade Unions
Intersind	Confederation of Industries (Public Sector)
UIL	Unione Italiana di Lavoro / Italian Union of Labor

WFTU   World Federation of Trade Unions

Government Holding Companies and Other Agencies

ENEL   Ente Nazionale di Energia
                        Elettrica / National Electric Power
                        Agency
ENI   Ente Nazionale Idrocarburi / National
                        Hydrocarbons Agency
IMI   Istituto Mobiliare Italiano / Italian Real
                        Estate Investment Bank
IRI   Istituto di Ricostruzione
                        Industriale / Institute for Industrial
                        Reconstruction
ISTAT   Istituto Centrale di Statistica / Central
                        Statistical Institute
RAI   Radiotelevisione Italiana / Italian
                        Radio and Television Company

CHRONOLOGY

April 29, 1945	World War II ends in Italy.
June 2, 1946	In a referendum, the Italian people choose a republic over the monarchy.
May, 1947	Communist and Socialist Parties ejected from the cabinet.
January 1, 1948	New republican constitution goes into effect.
April 18, 1948	First parliamentary election produces a major Christian Democratic victory.
1949	Italy joins NATO.
1952	Italy joins the European Coal and Steel Community.
1956-1959	Socialists and Communists diverge. Communists announce their program of the "Italian Way to Socialism."
1959-1963	The opening to the left emerges.
December, 1963	First center-left coalition government formed.
October, 1966	Socialists and Social Democrats temporarily united. Split again in July, 1969.
1968-1969	Eruption of the student movement.
October-December, 1969	"Hot Autumn" of the labor movement.
December, 1969	Emergence of terrorist violence.
Summer, 1970	Beginning of economic slowdown. Establishment of regular regional governments.
September, 1973	Berlinguer proposes the historic compromise.
October, 1973	Oil embargo with drastic

	increase in petroleum prices. Beginning of double-digit inflation.
May, 1974	Divorce referendum upholds the divorce law.
January, 1975	Socialists finally pull out of the center-left coalition.
June, 1975	Big Communist gains in the regional and local elections lead to a substantial increase in leftist governments below the national level.
June, 1976	These gains are repeated in parliamentary elections.
August, 1976	Andreotti forms a cabinet dependent on the abstention of the Communists and other parties. The PCI receives several important posts in Parliament.
March, 1978	Communists and Socialists become part of the majority supporting the government.
March-May, 1978	Aldo Moro kidnapped and then assassinated by Red Brigade terrorists.
January, 1979	Communists withdraw from the parliamentary majority, bringing down the government.
June, 1979	Communist vote declines in parliamentary elections for the first time.
March, 1980	Socialists join the government, re-creating the center-left coalition.
October, 1980	New four-party center-left coalition. The Socialists and Social Democrats agree to collaborate in the formulation of policy.

A POLITICAL HISTORY OF
POSTWAR ITALY

1

BACKGROUND

Postwar Italy has exhibited a remarkable combination of dynamism and immobility. Dynamism enabled the country to overcome the material damages of the Second World War rapidly. Immobility has existed, to a great extent, in the psychology of the people and particularly in the minds of the country's intellectuals and political commentators. In a number of respects the practicing politicians have been ahead of their associates who provided the conceptual frameworks that were supposed to explain their behavior. This does not mean that they were, or are, prepared to deal with the problems of modern Italian life. It does mean that they are relatively less rigid than the general public, but constrained by the necessity of attracting mass support in a system of competitive party politics.

The war ended with a part of Italy in ruins, but not the industrialized northwest. Transportation and communication networks had been severely damaged, public services needed massive reconstruction, and food and raw materials were in short supply. Northern industry, however, had survived, and small quantities of raw materials were even available to begin production. A continuing supply would be required to keep the factories operating steadily.

United States policy toward Italy was critical for economic revival. For political reasons the Americans desired a stable Italy that would not be vulnerable to a takeover by extremist political forces. Relief and reconstruction were considered essential to political stability. Since the United States was the least hostile of the many countries that had been the victims of Mussolini's foreign policy, and since the United States was the only major combatant to emerge from World War II with its economy strengthened rather

1

than wrecked, its 1944 commitment to Italian reconstruction provided one of the essentials for Italy's revival.[1] A second essential was the Italian capacity for hard work. And a third was the unity of the postwar Italian political leadership behind the goal of reconstruction. This unity began to break down in 1947, but in the immediate aftermath of the war it had enabled the country to change peacefully from a monarchy to a republic and to produce a constitution for this new republic.[2] The Christian Democratic (DC), Socialist (PSI), and Communist (PCI) Parties, the largest of the many postwar Italian parties, found the necessary minimum consensus to absorb the peace settlement without an internal rupture or collapse.

Fascist Italy had entered the war as an enemy of the United Nations Allies, and post-Fascist Italy ended the war as a cobelligerent of these same Allies. In the eyes of the Italians the period of cobelligerency erased the earlier period of enmity. The European victims of Fascist aggression, however, demanded punishment. U.S. efforts to ameliorate punitive terms had only partial success. On the whole, the peace treaty with Italy was a mild one, even if the Italians did not think so. Italy was required to pay reparations to the Eastern European victims of Fascist aggression and to Ethiopia, but the reparations were paid out of U.S. economic aid. Italy lost its colonies in Africa and in the eastern Mediterranean, thereby being spared the agonies of decolonization later suffered by France, Great Britain, and Portugal. It obtained a ten-year trusteeship over Italian Somaliland and wasted precious resources during the period. Italy was partially disarmed and demilitarized, but a few years after joining the North Atlantic Treaty Organization (NATO) in 1949 it was rearmed. Its territorial borders in Europe remained untouched except for the loss of a few valleys in the Alps on the French border and for the larger losses of eastern Venezia Giulia and the Istrian peninsula, including adjacent small islands. The city of Trieste and its hinterland were to become a free territory. Because of the Allies' inability to construct a government for this free territory, the area was divided in 1954. The Italians received administrative control over the city while the Yugoslavs obtained control over the hinterland. The loss of the undoubtedly Italian towns on the west coast of the Istrian peninsula was the only lasting injustice that the peace treaty imposed on the Italian nation. Similarly, the Italian retention of the South Tyrol might be considered the lasting injustice imposed on Austria, for over 60 percent of the population was German speaking.[3]

All the political parties that dominated the scene after the war had pre-Fascist roots. (The new, small wartime Action Party had disintegrated in 1946.) The DC had psychological, emotional, and doctrinal affiliations with the Catholic world and the Vatican. It was a heterogeneous collection of groups with differing views, held together by their religious identification, their thirst for power, and their suspicion of the Marxists. The PSI was divided after the war, as it had been before Fascism, between maximalist and reformist socialist groups. It was linked to the PCI by a Unity of Action Pact, first negotiated in 1934 by leaders of the two parties in exile, broken in 1939 in the aftermath of the Nazi-Soviet Non-Aggression Pact, and then renewed in 1941 after the German attack on the Soviet Union. The PCI was an important member of the international Communist movement with strong ties to Moscow. In the postwar period under the leadership of Palmiro Togliatti, the PCI pursued the domestic strategy of establishing a broad alliance with all "popular" forces, for example, the Socialists and Christian Democrats. Togliatti also constructed a mass party open to all sympathizers. He rejected the concept of a small cadre party limited to revolutionary elitists who would be believing Marxist-Leninists. The election of a constituent assembly on June 2, 1946, under the principle of proportional representation, confirmed the leading position held by the three parties. In round numbers the DC got 35 percent of the votes, the PSI 20 percent, the PCI 19 percent, with the remainder scattered among a number of minor parties.

The new constitution was completed at the end of 1947 and went into effect on January 1, 1948. It was an amalgam of liberal, Catholic, and Marxist doctrines in uneasy juxtaposition. It established a polity based on the principles of parliamentary democracy, universal adult suffrage, civil rights and legal protections, and extensive decentralization of the highly unitary state. It provided guarantees for the family and for the Catholic Church through the inclusion of the Lateran Accords of 1929. It recognized the existing mixed economy but left possibilities open for further socialization of economic enterprises. Many years were to pass before several sections of the constitution were effected and some parts have not yet become operative. The Constitutional Court and the Supreme Council of the Judiciary did not come into existence until 1956. The regular regional governments were created only in 1970. The law applying the right of referendum was finally passed shortly before the first referendum (on divorce) was held in 1974.

During the gestation period of the new republic and its constitution the Italian government was based on a coalition of parties forged by the Committees of National Liberation that had been recognized by the Allies during the war. Dependent on U.S. economic aid, the government sought to adjust its domestic policies to Western influences and preferences. This meant opening up the economy to international commerce, a reversal of the economic nationalism and autarchy of the late Fascist period. It meant encouraging private enterprise in the sectors of the economy not already under government ownership or control. The emergence of the Cold War in full force produced terrible strains within the Italian governing coalition. The first half of 1947 was the critical period. Under the pressure of the Greek civil war and Soviet demands on Turkey, the United States committed itself through the Truman Doctrine to a long-run and thoroughgoing involvement in the affairs of the European and Mediterranean worlds. Its anti-Soviet crusade would be directed also against all allies of the Soviet Union.

The Greek crisis had a sharp impact on internal Italian politics. In January 1947 the reformist wing of the PSI, under the leadership of Giuseppe Saragat, demanded that the party break the Unity of Action Pact with the PCI. The failure to achieve this demand led the reformists to secede and to establish a new party, later named the Italian Social Democratic Party (PSDI). During the same month the prime minister, Alcide De Gasperi of the DC, returned from a visit to Washington with a major loan from the U.S. Some say that he also brought back instructions to throw the PCI and PSI out of his cabinet, but there is no documentary evidence for this charge.[4] In any case, in May De Gasperi forced these two parties out of the government. In the summer Italy accepted the invitation to participate in the Marshall Plan. Togliatti approved but under Soviet pressure he was forced to reverse himself and direct the PCI in a struggle against the Plan. The PSI followed the Communist lead.

Matters came to a climax in the spring of 1948 with the election of the first parliament under the new constitution. The PCI and PSI forged a joint electoral ticket. In February 1948 a Communist coup d'état in Czechoslovakia heated the atmosphere in Italy. The Vatican and the Civic Committees of the Catholic Action Society threw themselves into the election campaign. The United States and its British and French allies supported the Christian Democrats. The election of April 18, 1948, was a major victory for the DC, which obtained over 48 percent of the popular vote and an absolute victory in the Chamber of Deputies and the Senate, the only time this would ever happen. The joint PCI-PSI slate received 31 percent of the vote, with the PCI dominating their parliamentary delegations numerically. Although the DC had a majority, De Gasperi formed a four-party cabinet with the small Social Democratic, Liberal (PLI), and Republican (PRI) Parties as partners. This centrist coalition would survive in various versions until the late 1950s.

The continuing Cold War rivalries began to work their way through Italian society during 1949. In 1944 a new united trade union confederation, the Italian General Confederation of Labor (CGIL), had been established under tripartite PCI, PSI, and DC leadership. The Communists and Socialists now used CGIL as a weapon in the struggle against implementation of the Marshall Plan. As a result, Christian Democratic, Social Democratic, and Republican trade unionists broke away in 1949 and shortly afterward established two new confederations: the Italian Confederation of Workers' Unions (CISL), nominally nonparty but actually DC dominated, and the Italian Union of Labor (UIL), led by Social Democratic and Republican trade unionists. U.S. financing helped to put and keep the new confederations on their feet.

The same year Italy was invited to join NATO. The PCI and PSI opposed Italian membership. The DC and PSDI were both internally divided. Attitudes favoring neutralism were widespread among large sectors of the public. Vatican intervention helped overcome internal DC resistance, however, and Italy joined.

The period of postwar economic and political revival came to a close in 1949. The consequences of a lost war had been absorbed. The economy was producing at higher than prewar levels. The country was committed to the Western world and was a member of all existing regional organizations of that world. Most of the institutions of the parliamentary republic were established and working. The cabinet coalition was relatively stable with a clear majority in parliament. The left opposed the system and the policy choices it made but had no option except to work within it.

A period of economic growth of a sort unknown before in the history of Italy was initiated in 1950. It was Italy's second industrial revolution, far broader and deeper than the first, which had occurred before World War I. At the beginning, however, no one knew what was to come. Surmounting the consequences of the war stimulated political and economic unrest based on increasing expectations. In the south peasant turbulence included the seizure of land belonging to huge, partially worked estates. In response the government produced its first major agricultural reform legislation. Anticipating permanent rural overpopulation, the government divided the estates into tiny farms and distributed them to as many landless peasants as possible. Naturally there was not enough land for all claimants. Administrative agencies, which became political plums, were established to help the new proprietors become more effective farmers through loans, training, and supplies.

Reform in the south was not limited to agriculture. In 1950 the

Southern Italy Fund (Cassa per il Mezzogiorno) was created. Its purposes were to break the age-old isolation and backwardness through a construction program of roads, dams, aqueducts, and irrigation systems. These were built in the hope that industry and commerce would enter in the wake of the public improvements. Tax credits, easy loans, and other favors were offered to encourage private investment. The growth of industry in the south was slow, however, and in 1956 the role of the government was expanded to include direct investment in and construction of industrial plants by public sector firms. Many of these new plants were large and capital intensive, requiring tremendous amounts of money while creating comparatively few new jobs. The expectation was that smaller and secondary industries, commerce, and services would grow around them. The failure of these expectations earned the huge public sector plants the name "cathedrals in the desert." The major exception was in the provinces just south of Rome where proximity to the capital encouraged a burgeoning of small and medium-sized plants.

The big growth of the Italian economy took place in the northwest regions where industry was already well established. Based on the modernization of existing plant, the construction of new factories using the most advanced technology, and a plentiful supply of cheap labor, the economy took off in a major spurt. The boom in the other Western European economies and in the United States created or expanded markets for Italian exports. The relatively low cost of raw materials that Italy imported and the reduction of trade barriers in the postwar world brought Italy into the mainstream of international trade. The country joined the European Coal and Steel Community and the General Agreement on Tariffs and Trade (GATT). The government also moved quickly to promote the growth of mass tourism.

The economy did not grow in the early 1950s as fast as the labor force, so unemployment rose. As economic development accelerated in the last half of the decade, unemployment then declined and a major exodus from the land began. Urban jobs meant large-scale commuting along with population transfers from the countryside to neighboring cities. Toward the end of the decade southern peasants began moving in large numbers to the northwest industrial regions to seek jobs in expanding industry and commerce. The emergence of labor shortages in the booming economies of Western Europe and North America stimulated Italian emigration, both permanent and on short-term contract. Marginal farms were abandoned. The Green Plan (Plano verde) of 1959 encouraged concentration of landholdings, reversing the earlier land reform legislation that had broken up the large estates.

Economic growth would produce visible results over a period of years. In the short run centrist government coalitions felt the strains and stresses of a country undergoing change and were divided among themselves. Local elections in 1950 and 1951 indicated declines in the strength of the centrist parties. The Christian Democrats came under increasing pressure from the Vatican and the Civic Committees of the Catholic Action Society to abandon their moderate centrist allies and form a stable coalition with the Monarchists and neo-Fascists.* De Gasperi successfully resisted these pressures in 1951 and 1952. Before the 1953 parliamentary elections the centrist coalition, anticipating the loss of its solid majority, changed the election law to permit the alliance that gained 50 percent plus one of the popular vote to obtain almost two-thirds of the seats in parliament. The PCI and PSI baptized it the "swindle law" and fought the election campaign on this issue. A minority of outraged centrists abandoned their own parties to form dissident slates. Their defection was decisive.

In the 1953 election the centrist coalition failed to obtain its needed popular majority by less than 1 percent. The DC vote fell to about 40 percent while its allies lost proportionately more. The centrist coalition still retained a slight majority of the seats in parliament, for proportional representation is never perfect. The gainers were the extremes: Monarchists and neo-Fascists, Socialists and Communists. This time the PSI ran independently of the PCI. De Gasperi's political career was at an end. He retired from politics and a year later he was dead.

During the election campaign the Socialist leader, Pietro Nenni, had suggested that his party might be available for an "opening to the left," that is, a coalition extending from the DC to the PSI. Although De Gasperi considered the suggestion premature, it was the first step in the disintegration of the Unity of Action Pact between Socialists and Communists. By 1955 the Socialists were hinting that their opposition to NATO was diminishing. In 1956 Nikita Khrushchev's revelations of the crimes of the Stalin era in the Soviet Union and the later Soviet invasion of Hungary widened the gap between the Italian Marxist parties. The PCI, although extremely uncomfortable, continued to defend the Soviet Union, while the PSI denounced Soviet behavior at home and abroad. Shortly

---

*The Monarchist Party was formed ostensibly to restore the monarchy to Italy. Actually, it was less a legitimist party than a protest party, cultivating southern revindication against the rest of the country. In subsequent years it split, reunited, and split again. The neo-Fascist party was the Movimento Sociale Italiano (MSI), or Italian Social Movement. Its inspiration was the Fascist Social Republic created by Mussolini behind the German lines in October 1943.

afterward, Nenni and Saragat explored the possibility of reuniting the PSI and the PSDI. The talks failed. Communist defense of the Soviet Union cost the PCI some prominent intellectuals, but there were no mass defections. Togliatti publicly advanced the idea of polycentrism, an idea that made no headway in the international Communist movement and that was soon withdrawn. He announced openly, however, that his party would pursue an "Italian way to socialism" that would be a democratic way. The following year he declared that his party alone determined its own policy line. For the Italian Communists the twin concepts of the Soviet Union as the guiding state and the Communist Party of the Soviet Union (CPSU) as the guiding party were finished.

With increasing difficulty De Gasperi's successors struggled to maintain the centrist coalition. Frequent political collapses led to minority governments that were dependent for their survival on abstentions by other parties, often from the right wing. The social reformist urge of the immediate postwar years had dissipated in the early 1950s. In 1954 Amintore Fanfani became secretary-general of the DC and embarked on a major effort to build up the party's bureaucratic structure to make it more independent of flanking groups like the Catholic Church or the Catholic Action Society. Gradually, he began to shift the political center of gravity toward the left, incurring the increasing suspicion of such business organizations as the Confederation of Industries (Confindustria) as well as church organizations and the smaller conservative parties. The 1955 election of the Christian Democrat, Giovanni Gronchi, as president of the republic was also identified as a shift to the left within the DC. The resistance by moderate party factions and outside interest groups limited the degree of movement. Although Fanfani and Gronchi were charged by some of their conservative colleagues with being enemies of private property, in fact during the last half of the 1950s business was flourishing. The major state-controlled firms, most of which were grouped into two large government-owned super-holding corporations, the Institute for Industrial Reconstruction (IRI) and the National Hydrocarbons Agency (ENI), were also expanding, particularly in the south. The Ministry of State Participations was created to exercise overall supervision of the public-sector businesses. The ministry had little effective control in fact, and IRI and ENI functioned autonomously, exercising political influence on parties and factions within parties.

Fanfani and Gronchi were also accused of being tepid toward Italy's commitments to the Atlantic community, if not actually neutralist and hostile. In practice, Italy was trading with any country in any part of the world, disregarding ideological or political labels. The decline of the old colonial system opened up opportunities for trade with new countries that had formerly been part of the protected markets of the European colonial powers. Also, the thaw in the Cold War improved trading possibilities with Soviet bloc countries. Nevertheless, Italy's major political and economic links remained with the countries of the Western world. These links were strengthened further when in 1957 Italy signed and ratified the three treaties establishing the European Economic Community (EEC), the European Investment Bank, and Euratom. The PSI abstained in the vote on the EEC and voted in favor of the other two organizations. The PCI opposed all three. For all practical purposes the Unity of Action Pact was now dead. Later, CGIL was to endorse the European Economic Community. In 1962 the Communists publicly shifted their position to come out in favor of the Common Market. So Italy, instead of becoming more neutralist, in fact became more than ever involved with its Atlantic partners.

In domestic affairs the late 1950s witnessed the implementation of a number of constitutional agencies. In 1956 the Constitutional Court was finally created. It immediately began to exercise its power to review the constitutionality of laws and decrees. Italy has no strong constitutional tradition so the new court had to proceed cautiously in checking parliament, the parties, or the cabinet. In the exercise of its power of judicial review, it generally upheld the civil and political rights of individuals and groups, and usually supported the central government in controversies with special regional governments.*

In 1958 the Superior Council of the Magistracy was established to exercise control over the judges of the regular courts: their appointment, assignment and transfer, promotion, and discipline. These were powers traditionally exercised by the Ministry of Justice, which was a political organ. To promote judicial independence the constitution provided for the creation of the new agency, but the various governments and parliaments took ten years to implement these constitutional provisions.

The era of the centrist cabinets was coming to an end with the approach of the parliamentary elections of 1958. Fanfani, as secretary-general of the DC, decided to move his party leftward

---

*Special regional governments were created for Sicily, Sardinia, Val d'Aosta, Trentino-Alto Adige, and later Friuli-Venezia Giulia. These areas had linguistic minorities or else had been the sites of separatist movements, factors that led to the concession of limited autonomy for the five regions.

cautiously, while continuing an anti-Communist barrage. An approach to the Socialists was being prepared, but it had to be done without exposing the DC to attacks from its more conservative members and supporters. The results of the election on May 25, 1958, appeared to justify Fanfani's strategy. Both the DC and the PSI gained votes and parliamentary seats compared to 1953. The Communist vote remained stable in spite of the shocks produced in the international Communist movement by the events of 1956. The Monarchists and neo-Fascists lost votes. Within the DC and Socialist Parties the factions favoring an opening to the left gained strength. A new alternative to the stalemate of recent years appeared feasible.

Fanfani formed a coalition with the Social Democrats. Conservative objections within his own party and left-wing resistance within the PSI made a real center-left coalition impossible. Opposition emerged within the DC to Fanfani's attempts to consolidate control of the party by the bureaucracy that he dominated. Flanking groups resisted his strategy of reducing their impact on party affairs. In short order his leadership was threatened, and in January 1959 his government was brought down by opponents inside his own party, who were supported by Vatican prelates and leaders of the Catholic Action Society. Fanfani resigned as secretary-general of the DC.

Antonio Segni formed a minority DC cabinet dependent on the support of the small conservative Liberal and Monarchist Parties. Aldo Moro replaced Fanfani as secretary-general of the DC but made no attempt to reconstruct a tight party organization. Factions, or *correnti*, as the Italians call them, flourished again and in subsequent years became parties within the party, each with its own organization, its own offices, its own press and publications services, and its own finances. A similar evolution was occurring in the other parties, with the important exception of the PCI.

Segni's minority government provided little more than routine caretaker administration. It rebuffed Austrian-backed efforts by the German-speaking majority in the South Tyrol (Alto Adige) toward regional autonomy for the province of Bolzano.* Anti-Italian demonstrations in the South Tyrol became more extreme, degenerating in the 1960s into acts of terrorism. Not until 1969 was an agreement reached between Italy and Austria granting the provincial government of Bolzano more functions, although not the separate status of an autonomous region.

The recognition by Christian Democratic national leaders such

---

*Bolzano was tied to the Italian province of Trento in the special region of Trento-Alto Adige.

as Moro and Fanfani that center or center-right coalitions no longer had a majority in parliament or in the country renewed interest in an opening to the Socialists. In the spring of 1960 the conservative parties that had upheld Segni's *monocolore* government withdrew their support. The government resigned, initiating a crisis that lasted for months and threatened the existence of democracy in Italy. Moro began negotiations for a new cabinet composed of the Christian Democratic, Social Democratic, and Republican Parties. Since these parties lacked a majority in parliament, he indicated a willingness to accept the abstention of the Socialist Party, which would enable a new government to survive. The Socialist price was the nationalization of the electric power industry. Conservative Catholic opposition to this indirect opening to the left mounted. As a result, another DC minority caretaker government was constructed, led by Fernando Tambroni, a former minister of the interior. When it became apparent the cabinet's survival was dependent on the votes of the neo-Fascist MSI, several cabinet ministers resigned. For the first time since the fall of Fascism the heirs of Mussolini were in a position of potential crucial leverage at the national level.* Tambroni submitted his government's resignation and Fanfani made new efforts to reach an agreement with the Socialists, but Vatican cardinals intervened to veto the move. Fanfani gave up and President Gronchi rejected Tambroni's resignation, instructing him to fill the vacancies in his cabinet. To justify the clerical intervention an unsigned editorial was published in the Vatican newspaper, *L'Osservatore romano*, claiming that collaboration with the Socialists was incompatible in principle with Catholic doctrine and insisting that Catholics were bound by the guidance and instructions of the hierarchy.[5]

The prime minister proceeded to convert his caretaker government into a politically active one and to curry support with a wide variety of groups in Italian society. Fears of his intentions fanned tensions within the left-wing opposition. The plan for an MSI congress to be held in Genoa at the end of June provoked anti-Fascist riots in the city that spread to other parts of Italy. Tambroni was forced to suspend the permit for the MSI congress. In retaliation the neo-Fascists withdrew their support of the cabinet. The executive bureau (*direzione*) of the DC forced Tambroni to resign. The stage was now set for Moro and Fanfani to renew the effort for an opening to the left.[6]

The DC leaders moved carefully. They were aided by the new

---

*At the local level a number of municipal governments, especially in the south, included the MSI or were dependent on its support.

pope, John XXIII, who began to insert his influence in church-state relations after the Tambroni crisis. In effect, he gradually lifted the Vatican veto against the DC approach to the Socialists. The PSI cooperated by agreeing to abstain when Fanfani formed a one-party cabinet of "democratic restoration," as he called it. In 1961 center-left governments were formed in several of the major cities and provinces in central and northern Italy. The normal formula was a coalition of Christian Democrats, Social Democrats, Republicans, and Socialists. At the same time other local governments of the center-right, center, and left (PCI-PSI) continued to exist. Resistance to the new formula was strong, but declining, in both Catholic and Socialist camps. The left wing of the PSI still preferred collaboration with the PCI to participation in bourgeois coalitions. At the international level opposition to the center-left evaporated when the new U.S. president, John F. Kennedy, informally indicated to Fanfani that he would not object.

The principal Socialist demand had been the nationalization of the electric power industry. Moro and Fanfani were able to carry most of their party with them in meeting this demand. In early 1962 Fanfani formed a three-party (DC, PSDI, PRI) cabinet that received a "favorable" abstention from the PSI. During the summer this government introduced the bill to nationalize the electric power industry. Passage of the bill in the autumn laid the groundwork for the election campaign of the spring of 1963. From the right the DC was accused of betraying the country; from the left the PSI was attacked for selling the workers out to the class enemy.

The parliamentary election held on April 28, 1963, produced substantial gains in the popular vote of the Liberals and Communists, both opposed to the center-left. The PSI suffered a slight loss and the DC a substantial one. These losses temporarily delayed the evolution of the proposed coalition, and another caretaker cabinet was formed. It lasted until the end of the year. In December a four-party government was created under Aldo Moro's leadership. For the first time since 1947 the Socialists entered the cabinet. Pietro Nenni became deputy prime minister. In January 1964 the leftist factions within the PSI abandoned their party to form the Italian Socialist Party of Proletarian Unity (PSIUP). It followed the PCI in its opposition to the coalition, while Liberals, Monarchists, and Missini (as MSI members are known) opposed the coalition from the right.

Throughout the long period of political travail, the economy had been expanding. During the years from 1959 to 1963 the rate of Italian economic growth was second only to that of Japan. The inception of the Common Market in January 1958 had reinforced the development of the earlier years. By 1963 the gross national product in real terms was 138 percent of the 1958 figure. New investment was averaging 25 percent of GNP per year. The expansion was particularly marked in industry and services, less so in agriculture. Foreign trade and tourism boomed, the result of general prosperity abroad. At home mass ownership of automobiles and the new network of superhighway toll roads transformed the life styles of the Italian people, breaking down the isolation of one region from another, reducing provincialism and localism.

During this five-year period 1.38 million people abandoned agriculture, approximately double the number that had fled the land during the previous decade. The exodus went out from all over rural Italy, but particularly from the south. The social dislocations created by these large-scale migrations were borne not only by the migrants but by the ill-prepared cities that received them. The expansion of urban areas and populations exerted heavy pressures on inadequate housing, educational, and public service structures.

As essentially full employment was reached, for the first and only time in Italian history, wages rose. The growth of domestic demand for goods and services led to price rises and to an expansion of imports, which caused balance of payments difficulties. The combination of inflation and a shaky lira induced the government to impose credit and monetary restrictions. These brought the economic miracle to a halt at the end of 1963, just when the four-party center-left coalition was being organized. The slowdown of the economy between 1963 and 1965 was then used for political purposes to justify the postponement of a number of reforms the Socialists had demanded as their price for joining the cabinet. Establishment of governments for the regular regions of Italy was put off until an unspecified later date. Inauguration of national programming (indicative, not command) was postponed until the economy would revive.

A parliamentary act of 1964 provided for the gradual abolition of sharecropping (*mezzadria*). As existing contracts expired, the landowner would have to sell, with the sharecropper having the first option to buy. Low-interest government loans would be available to enable the sharecropper to buy the land and necessary equipment and supplies. Thus, in the course of the next decade an age-old rural institution gradually disappeared, and a new group of peasant proprietors was created. In central Italy, where sharecropping had been prominent and where the sharecroppers had provided much of the rural support for the PCI and PSI, the change in land tenure arrangements did not produce a change in voting patterns. In fact, the support for the left increased.

The following spring the government issued a decree incorporating a wide range of antirecession measures. Credit was eased; money was pumped into the economy through public works programs and expanded social welfare benefits. The effects of these stimulants became visible later in the year.

The year 1965 marked the twentieth anniversary of the end of the Second World War. Italy was no longer the provincial, backward, and autarchic country of the Fascist period. It was one of the advanced industrialized countries of the world, although it contained zones of underdevelopment. Inequalities in income and status continued, but all sectors of society were better off than ever before. Even the poor were less poor, in absolute if not in relative terms. The second industrial revolution had ruptured the old static social structure; geographically and sociologically, society was more mobile. More young people were in school, and they were staying there longer.

The political institutions of the parliamentary republic were in difficulty, but were surviving the pressures of rapid social and economic change. Age-old rivalries between clericals and anticlericals were being moderated, if not eliminated. In operation and in programs the political parties and the administrative structures of the government lagged behind the times. Old dogmas were under challenge, but far from dead. Among the people, old behavior patterns of indifference to social and civic obligations persisted at the same time that political consciousness was growing. The geographic mobility, the spread of radio and television, and the increase in school attendance were creating a people that was becoming similar in outlook and aspiration to the peoples in the advanced countries of Western Europe.

NOTES

1. James E. Miller, "The Search for Stability: An Interpretation of American Policy in Italy: 1943-1946," *The Journal of Italian History*, Spring 1978, pp. 264-86.

2. For an English translation of the text of the constitution see U.S., Department of State, *Documents and State Papers*, I, No. 1 (April 1948), 46-63.

3. The text of the peace treaty can be found in U.S., Department of State, *Treaty of Peace with Italy*, Treaties and Other International Acts Series 1648 (1947).

4. On this question see the article of Simon Serfaty, "International Anomaly: The U.S. and the Communist Parties in France and Italy," *Studies in Comparative Communism*, Spring-Summer 1975, pp. 123-46.

5. An English translation appears in *U.S. News and World Report*, May 30, 1960, pp. 73-74.

6. See K. Robert Nilsson, "Italy's 'Opening to the Right': The Tambroni Experiment of 1960" (Ph.D. dissertation, Columbia University, 1964).

2

ECONOMIC RECOVERY

The recession of 1963-65 was brief. Initiated in the autumn of 1963 when the Bank of Italy tightened credit controls, its effects were first felt in early 1964. Restrictive measures were introduced to protect the country's balance of payments and its foreign exchange reserves. The government borrowed from the International Monetary Fund (IMF) to check speculation and to protect the stability of the lira. A sharp drop in domestic demand curtailed the previous wage and price boom of the economic miracle. The rate of economic growth contracted. Gradual recovery began in early 1965, except in the construction and extractive industries, which took longer to come back.

The revived economic growth lasted through the end of the decade. It differed in nature from earlier periods of expansion. Investments began increasing in the spring of 1965, but grew more slowly than in the past, or even in comparison to other Western countries during these same years. Government spending gradually increased. The Bank of Italy cautiously expanded the money supply, but more to sustain than to stimulate renewed economic growth. At all costs, it wanted to avoid inflationary excesses and to stabilize the exchange rate of the lira. The economy achieved gains in productivity and particularly in exports. Between 1963 and 1969 exports more than doubled. Steady reductions of trade barriers within the European Community and favorable Italian prices in comparison to those of competitors explain much of this expansion. In addition, Italian producers engaged in a major export drive to compensate for the slower growth of internal demand.

The automobile boom continued. By the end of the decade Italy was almost as motorized as the most advanced countries of Western Europe. Stimulating and reinforcing this rapid increase, a government road construction program gave primary emphasis to superhighways and toll roads. Smaller appropriations were directed to the extension and improvement of the ordinary road system. In the early 1970s Italy had a superhighway network that was a close second to that of West Germany. Public transportation, both urban and interurban, remained relatively neglected. The cities were jammed with cars. Meanwhile the railroads carried a declining proportion of passenger and freight traffic.

Employment had fallen during the brief setback and recovered only gradually. Productive capacity remained underutilized even after growth rates were resumed. At the end of 1969 industrial employment was only slightly above the 1963 level. At the same time the average industrial work week was somewhat reduced. The growth of production was the result of regular and continuing increases in hourly productivity.[1] Since additional workers were being added slowly, young people in search of jobs found few available. More students were staying in school longer, however, so that the labor force grew at a diminishing rate. In the south, furthermore, the slow growth of the economy discouraged many people, particularly women, from registering at the unemployment offices for jobs, or even from entering the labor force in the first place. At the same time the expansion of national pension systems encouraged retirements so that the industrial labor force was increasingly concentrated in the central age groups.

Labor costs gradually declined in the second half of the 1960s. A 1964 law transferring the costs of certain fringe benefits from the wage package to the public treasury reduced the employers' contributions to these social costs while increasing the burden on the public treasury. The salary increases achieved in the 1966 round of wage negotiations were moderate.* Put together with the required indexing of salaries to the cost of living (the scala mobile), which was also moderate because of the relative stability of prices, unit labor costs declined slightly. The increase in industrial productivity more than compensated for the increases in wages and fringe benefits. Raw material costs were stable or in decline, while wholesale prices rose slowly so that profits in private industry increased. Much of the profit was invested in reorganizing production and, to a lesser extent, in new technology. Another part was invested abroad. These were not the types of investments to create many new jobs in

---

* Italian labor contracts are normally made for a three-year period.

private industry. Had it not been for political pressure on public sector firms to expand employment, the growth of the industrial labor force would have been even slower. The excess labor foisted on public sector industries was one of the factors leading to their declining efficiency and reduced profits.

As surplus industrial capacity discouraged private investment, so did low interest rates. Both factors served to stimulate capital export in the late 1960s. At the end of the decade the Bank of Italy, realizing the consequences of its policy, raised internal interest rates to make domestic investment more attractive.

In that period industrial investment was concentrated in the public sector. IRI's and ENI's proportion of total investment increased regularly, making the economy more dependent on the public sector and on state subsidies granted to private firms. To a substantial degree new investment came from bank loans. The big expansion of fixed indebtedness would create difficult problems during the slowdown of the 1970s. The state issued bonds, bought mostly by government-controlled banks. Increasingly, the state provided direct grants to public sector firms for capital investment, to substitute for the scantiness of profits available for reinvestment, and to reduce the price of money. The Bank of Italy slowly lost control over the money supply.[2]

Other than industry, critical areas of the Italian economy remained relatively neglected. Agriculture was not modernized at a rate comparable to that of other member states of the EEC, nor was the food-processing industry improving in efficiency. Public investments in education, sanitation, public transportation, and housing were insufficient. Italy was extremely competitive with other countries in the production and sale of consumer goods requiring medium-level technology but weak in those dependent on advanced technology. Both public and private sectors of industry preferred to buy the results of applied research done in other countries, through licensing and royalty agreements, rather than to set up research laboratories on a large scale in Italy. The failure to make research and development an important part of the educational-scientific enterprise and the low level of support for basic research resulted in a brain drain of young scientists and technologists who found better opportunities abroad. In the long run this neglect reduced the competitive position of the economic system.

The pattern in growth and distribution of firms shifted. The total number of industrial workers remained stable, but after 1966 the proportion working in big firms (over 500 employees) began to decline while the proportion in medium-sized (between 100 and 500 employees) and small industries (fewer than 100 employees) grew. Greater specialization made the smaller units flexible and profitable. The large number of tiny shops (employing fewer than ten) of an artisan and handicraft nature, always present on the Italian scene, continued to survive.

These tiny operations had always been prominent in the commercial and services sectors. With the overall stability of the industrial labor force, with the continuing exodus of manpower from agriculture, and with the expansion of the working-age population, it is not surprising that the services sector was under pressure to absorb the demand for jobs. In the late 1960s the major portion of the limited growth in national employment occurred here and in public administration. In neither area, however, did expansion contribute to efficiency. The center-left governments of the period had put on their agenda the reform of the public administration and the reform of the markets and distribution networks in Italy. Pressures to expand jobs in these sectors, however, led to poor service in the public administration and high retail prices. Naturally, general discontent rose among the people, who, if unable to get much for their money in the way of goods and services, then demanded higher wages and salaries.

A major formal goal of the center-left coalition was the establishment of a system of national planning to give direction and coherence to economic growth. The development of a five-year plan was a principal Socialist condition for joining the government. Because the new coalition came into existence in a period of economic slowdown, Moro had successfully persuaded the Socialists that recovery was necessary before new experiments could be introduced. With the recovery of 1965, Socialist pressure for planning became the prime issue of the political debate.[3]

The DC had committed itself to planning, but was cautious and hesitant about implementing its promise. Its election losses of 1963 had often been attributed to the reform commitment as well as to the 1962 nationalization of the electric power industry. A large portion of the rank-and-file party members and of the DC electorate had opposed the opening to the left in any case, and these political considerations were additional reasons for DC politicians to proceed slowly. To make the experiment more palatable to a suspicious electorate, they avoided the word "planning" and substituted the word "programming." Planning, especially on a five-year basis, had too many Marxist and bolshevik associations. In addition, the programming was supposed to be democratic, although nobody knew precisely what the phrase "democratic programming" really meant. Generically, it was supposed to mean participation. But by whom?

Legislation in 1965 created an interministerial committee to supervise and approve the first five-year program for 1966-70. This committee of the economic ministers was chaired by the minister of the budget. The programming machinery was located in the Budget Ministry. An advisory committee of experts was formed to give technical advice to the cabinet ministers as well as to oversee the programming operations. The technical committee proved to be a most political body, composed of representatives from the major industrial, commercial, and agricultural trade associations, from the principal trade union confederations, plus a number of university economists. Even the economists, however, had party identifications. Consequently, the program that emerged was more a result of political bargaining than a scientific product of the best economic and statistical minds in Italy. This was participatory democratic programming.

The five-year plan was finally passed by parliament in early 1967. The basic goals of the program were five: (1) to produce a growth of national income to achieve full employment at higher levels of well-being; (2) to increase agricultural productivity to meet the growing domestic demand for foodstuffs and to expand exports; (3) to reduce the gap between agricultural and nonagricultural incomes and to eliminate underemployment in agriculture; (4) to create new jobs in the south outside agriculture, particularly in industry; and (5) to expand investment in the public services—education, health, scientific research, and public transportation—without at the same time blocking all expansion of private consumption. There were no annual quotas, no specific production goals by economic sector; instead the five years were treated as a whole and the goals were set in the form of average percentage increases. The following projections of average annual growth, widely divorced from reality, were developed:

Industrial production—7 percent
Agricultural production—2.85 percent
Services—4.5 percent
Public administration—3.65 percent

It was expected that over the five-year period there would be a gradual increase in the proportion of the gross national product devoted to public as against private consumption; a higher share of national income would be allocated to health, education, and welfare. Underlying the program was the assumption that the pre-1964 rate of growth would be restored, and part of the increase in gross national product would be available to achieve these goals. A second underlying assumption was that the government and the public administration could function effectively, could organize and implement the necessary decisions, and could induce the required investments. Both assumptions were wrong.

When the program was published, Fanfani, a former prime minister and professor of economic history, called it a dream book. Before we laugh too hard at the dream book, however, we should reflect that this was a first attempt, that there was neither experience nor a political tradition or a civic culture to support the planning process.

During early discussions of planning, the imposition of obligatory programs had been rejected. By the time programming became a real political possibility, the private business community, the leaders of the public sector industries, and the DC party had already made it clear that at the most they would accept only indicative programming. The Socialists knew this when they entered the center-left coalitions but expected that the specific indicators for the future would be taken seriously. Since the underlying assumptions supporting the programming were erroneous—the resources were not available in sufficient quantity, nor was the political will or administrative effectiveness present—and since the indicators produced by the programming process were faulty, the program soon collapsed. Executives in both the private and public sectors continued to make decisions based on either market considerations or on whatever inducements were granted to them by the government on an ad hoc basis.

No second five-year program has yet appeared. The technical staff set up in the Budget Ministry has remained in existence, however, since in Italy no jobs are ever abolished; and it continues to produce a variety of studies, projections, and analyses that usually meet the fate of such exercises in all governments.

It would be wrong to conclude that the collapse of the programming effort left no benefits to Italian society. There were limited improvements in governmental budgetary procedures. For the first time one office in a single ministry was required to correlate its plans with another office in the same ministry. For the first time ministries were forced to think beyond the preparation of the next year's budget. The same held true for organized groups outside the government. The habit of depending on improvisation and ad hoc adjustment to events was disturbed slightly.

In the place of economic reform the Christian Democrats substituted the further expansion and colonization of the public sector industries. In effect, the attempt to make a more efficient socioeconomic system was abandoned in favor of a welfare economy: the concessions of grants, subsidies, and public expenditures to every claimant to the governmental largesse. Some claimants were naturally more favored than others. Most favored was a group that its critics called the "state bourgeoisie." Included in this group were executives and managers of the public sector industries and of government-controlled banks and financial holding companies, and the speculators and adventurers who put together large conglomerates with grants from the state and loans from these banks. The speculators made fortunes on the deals they promoted rather than on the productivity of the enterprises they controlled. They were supported by the government because they were supposed to promote economic growth, particularly in the south and in the islands. The legal basis of their operations was a 1965 law favoring industrial concentration. The preferred loci of their intervention were the chemical, petrochemical, and synthetic fibers industries.[4]

The speculators owed their fortunes to their close relations with the parties of the center-left coalition. They expressed their gratitude with financial contributions to these parties and to the factions and party leaders. They were shrewd enough not to neglect the opposition. Likewise, the executives and managers appointed to important positions in the public sector owed their appointments to their political associations. In the distribution of positions the Christian Democrats got the lion's share, but the Socialists also received a portion of the patronage; the two smaller parties of the coalition, Social Democratic and Republican, got the remaining crumbs. The state bourgeoisie were thus both beneficiaries and benefactors of the political system.

New factories were built and new jobs created, but the jobs in the plants were filled on the basis of political connections. Inadequate management, poor labor discipline, and mistaken product priorities did not make for profitable operations. Gradually in the late 1960s the deficits in the public sector began to increase. This sector had been reasonably effective and profitable in the 1950s and early 1960s. It had helped to stimulate the economic miracle and had supported the expansion of private industry and of exports. In the south, especially, the larger share of big business was in state-controlled firms. In the later 1960s, however, their qualitative decline contrasted with their quantitative growth. The costs of the qualitative decline would not become conspicuous until the 1970s when scandalous losses were revealed. Since jobs once created must be kept going at all costs, no big firm, private or public, is allowed to fail. So in the 1970s the banks would rescue the unprofitable operations.

Naturally not every public sector firm is unprofitable, nor is every executive or every worker unqualified. The scandals that made the newspaper headlines concentrated on the failures, not the successes. One prominent failure was the takeover of the huge Montedison chemical complex by a combination of IRI, ENI, and Istituto Mobiliare Italiano (IMI), a government investment bank. The rivals in these three government institutions first squeezed out the former private management of Montedison and then engaged in a power struggle for control among themselves that left the conglomerate floundering in a sea of debt.

Another failure was the decision taken in 1967 to construct an Alfa Romeo automobile plant (Alfa Sud) in the Naples area. Alfa Romeo is a public sector firm, part of the IRI group. Fiat, the largest private business in Italy, unsuccessfully opposed the project. The PSI supported the new plant, although it was not part of the five-year program. The PCI was persuaded to endorse it as a contribution to southern development, in spite of the Communist position ostensibly emphasizing mass over personal transportation. The government decision was based on the expected continuation of booming automobile demand. Numerous delays and bad planning postponed the completion of the plant until 1972. The political hiring policies and the lack of control over production lines meant that the first and every subsequent car manufactured by Alfa Sud has been produced at a loss. The current management now hopes that the plant may break even by 1983.

In the late 1950s the government decided to build a modern steel plant at Taranto, at the instep of the Italian boot. The plant began operations in 1964 and was successful. Because it made money, another decision was made in the late 1960s to double its size. By the time the addition was completed in 1974, a worldwide depression had hit the steel industry, so that this enlarged plant, along with others already in existence, was struggling to survive.

These examples illustrate a combination of bad policy, bad timing, and bad luck. This is not the whole story of the Italian economy in the last half of the 1960s, however. In the Veneto and Emilia-Romagna, for example, economic growth converted these regions from a semirural to a modern industrial and commercial society. To a lesser degree this was also true in Tuscany and Lazio. Here growth resulted from the initiative of many small and medium-sized firms, almost all of them private, many of them created by former peasants. This geographical expansion diluted the previous concentration of industry in the northwest industrial triangle—Genoa, Turin, and Milan. Here (except in southern Lazio) economic progress occurred without the special benefits and assistance of government agencies like the Southern Italy Fund. Many of these new operations were oriented to the then flourishing export market.

Government policies did not aid agriculture effectively. The establishment of the Common Agricultural Program (CAP) of the European Economic Community did no good for Italian agriculture or for Italian and other European consumers. The program subsidized the high prices and growing surpluses of dairy products and meat animals, foodstuffs produced in excess quantities in France, West Germany, and the Netherlands. Italy was a major importer of these products from its EEC partners, although it could have obtained them at lower prices outside the EEC. The Mediterranean fruits and vegetables produced by Italy received no comparable support. Through both higher prices and financial contributions Italy had to pay the cost to keep the CAP solvent. The Italian government made feeble efforts to change the rules. Acceptance of the unfair burden could be rationalized as the price for the gains the EEC provided in nonagricultural sectors.[5]

The EEC was not totally neglectful of Italian agriculture. Its grants to Italy for agricultural restructuring and development were underutilized because Italian public administration was too inefficient to exploit them properly. Italy's weak participation in European regional affairs and inadequate functioning at home cost both farmers and the citizenry at large a high price.

In spite of limited involvement in the regular functioning of European regional institutions, Italy did take some action to promote its political interests in Europe. It unsuccessfully supported British applications for entry into the EEC, but the French vetoes of the United Kingdom's requests for admission could not be overridden. British membership was no economic threat to Italian interests, and the Italians believed that the British could play a useful role in helping offset France-German domination of the community.

On an opposite tack the Italian government moved to block Austria's efforts to become associated with the EEC although it had no objection in principle to Austria's application for associate membership. Italy was engaged, however, in a dispute with the Vienna government over the South Tyrol. Austria was accused of permitting its territory to be used as a base by anti-Italian terrorists from the German-speaking Tyrolese inhabitants of the province of Bolzano and was also charged with encouraging separatist sentiment. Austria denied both accusations but did support the claims of the South Tyrol People's Party (SVP) that Italy was not living up to the stipulations of the De Gasperi-Gruber agreement of 1946, the accord that regulated Italian treatment of the German-speaking inhabitants. The dispute dragged on through most of the 1960s, with charges and countercharges, negotiations and collapses of negotiations. It was during one of these breakdowns that the Italians vetoed Austria's application to the EEC. In 1969 an agreement between Rome and Vienna was reached. The Italian government expanded the rights of the German-speaking Tyrolese and the powers of the Bolzano provincial government dominated by the SVP. The Italian veto of Austria's application for associate status in the EEC was withdrawn. Interestingly, throughout the whole period of the dispute there is no indication that trade between the two countries was affected.

The U.S.-Soviet joint presentation of the nuclear non-proliferation treaty raised a number of doubts in the Italian government, doubts spurred mainly, though not exclusively, by economic considerations. Renouncing the establishment of a nuclear weapons system did not bother Italians on the grounds of high politics. They had no illusions that they were, or could be, a great power, and they had no intention of investing in nuclear weapons. They did fear, however, that adherence ot the proposed treaty might deprive them of the economic benefits of the spinoff from military atomic research. They thought the treaty might interfere with their own peaceful nuclear research, thereby impairing economic growth and placing the country at a competitive disadvantage vis-à-vis the atomic powers. They also preferred that the inspection functions incorporated into the treaty be carried out by Euratom, an EEC organization, rather than by the United Nations International Atomic Energy Agency. In addition, Italians worried about the prospect of being potential victims of nuclear blackmail. All these considerations led Italy to delay acceptance of the treaty in 1966 and 1967.

Since other European countries, particularly West Germany, shared these same concerns, negotiations dragged on until 1968 before reaching a satisfactory conclusion that enabled Italy to adhere to the non-proliferation treaty. In that year the super-powers guaranteed the non-nuclear states that the benefits of nuclear research for peaceful purposes would be transferred to them. They also gave assurances against nuclear blackmail (for whatever these assurances are worth). A compromise was reached on inspection procedures whereby the International Atomic Energy Agency retained overall responsibility, but in Western Europe Euratom functioned as the operating agency of this United Nations organization.

Italy endorsed United Nations action to promote the economic development of Third and Fourth World countries. The governments of the center-left coalition made many rousing declarations of responsibility to the poorer nations of the world. The Socialist Party, in particular, asserted the moral responsibility of Italy and other Western countries. But these declarations and assertions produced little concrete assistance. Italy was engaged in a major effort to expand foreign commerce, an effort that included the underdeveloped countries, but it concentrated on trade, not aid. Of all the advanced, developed members of the Organization for Economic Cooperation and Development (OECD), Italy and Japan were and still are the two countries giving the lowest amount of foreign aid as a proportion of GNP. In its pursuit of trade Italy had established a commercial office in Peking in 1964 and had concluded trade agreements with the Communist government while maintaining formal diplomatic relations with the Nationalist government on Taiwan. In 1970 Italy broke with the Nationalists and gave de jure recognition to the Communist Chinese regime.

The year 1969 brought to an end twenty years of continuous economic growth that had transformed Italy in many ways but had left it vulnerable to future setbacks. The margins of flexibility of the economic system had been reduced. The country was more than ever a transformer of raw materials imported from abroad. It was increasingly an importer of foodstuffs and technological innovation. The state capitalism was neither robust nor efficient. National economic programming had failed. The early dynamism of its entrepreneurial leadership was dissipating. Its earlier advantages of low-cost labor and newly achieved economies of scale were ending. It still had widespread weak and backward sectors, in agriculture, in retail distribution, in investment goods, and in construction and real estate. These contradictions were to plague it throughout the next decade.

In the aftermath of the failure of economic programming, in the insufficient growth of the domestic economy, Italian commentators with a propensity for conspiracy theses found political explanations for the poor performance of the center-left governments. Since exports were increasing, there was no real danger of balance of payments crises. There was surplus capacity in various industries. The Bank of Italy had sustained and guaranteed the sale of treasury bonds to the banks and the investing public between 1966 and 1969, limiting the pressure on the treasury to expand the monetary base. Consequently there was little likelihood of significant price increases at home. Therefore, these analysts conclude, the Christian

Democrats held back on programming and stronger economic stimu-lants because the resulting sociopolitical changes could threaten their domination of Italian society. The welfare economy that they promoted instead consolidated DC hegemony, produced a solution to the exacerbated rivalries of party factions by providing them with patronage and financial support, kept the Socialists quiet by sharing some of the spoils, and postponed the hard decisions to another decade. The Socialists acquiesced, according to this interpretation, because they had been bought off.[6] They had fallen victim to the historic Italian vice of transformism.

This argument has some validity but is insufficient. It neglected some Italian economic history and certain current political necessi-ties. The Italian people, and the financial managers of the Bank of Italy in particular, still had an historic fear of inflation and of deficits in international accounts. This fear was an inheritance from the wild inflation of the late 1940s and the incipient inflation of the 1961-63 boom. The past preyed on the minds of the decision makers, who preferred not to run risks that might threaten the stability of the lira. The lira was to be defended; that was the prime objective. Furthermore, Moro never had strong support in his own camp for the reform program to which he was publicly committed; his position would have been undermined by his DC rivals if he had pushed faster and harder. In the next decade the priorities would be changed.

NOTES

1. Michele Salvati, *Il sistema economico italiano: Analisi di una crisi* (Bologna: Il Mulino, 1975), p. 41.

2. Mariano D'Antonio, *Sviluppo e crisi del capitalismo italiano 1951-1972* (Bari: De Donato, 1973), pp. 227-31.

3. Joseph LaPalombara, *Italy: The Politics of Planning*, National Planning Series, No. 7 (Syracuse: Syracuse University Press, 1966).

4. Giorgio Galli, *Storia della Democrazia Cristiana* (Bari: Laterza, 1978), pp. 249-66.

5. F. Roy Willis, *Italy Chooses Europe* (New York: Oxford University Press, 1971).

6. Galli, *Storia della Democrazia Christiana*, pp. 249-66.

3

THE ROLE OF
THE SOCIALISTS

The Socialists rationalized their entry into the center-left coalitions of the 1960s on both socioeconomic and political grounds. The reforms that they expected from the coalitions were supposed to transform Italian society by providing more social justice for more people. In the process the Communists would be isolated; the Socialists would attract large blocs of voters away from the PCI, and once more become the largest party of the left. Great numbers of formerly Communist voters would now shift to a party unequivocally committed to parliamentary democracy and the European and Atlantic communities. The Italian political system, therefore, would be strengthened as domestic political institutions gained a previously lacking legitimacy among the masses. The pro-Western foreign policies of the earlier centrist coalitions would be reinforced. Even the preeminent electoral position of the Christian Democrats could be threatened. A future alternation of governments was now possible, an alternation to provide flexibility and choice within the framework of democratic institutions.

These anticipations remained unrealized, but the center-left was far from the total failure later judgments assigned to it. The political isolation of the Communist Party remained incomplete. True, at the national level the PSI was in the government rather than in the opposition with the PCI, but the splinter Socialists who had created PSIUP in 1964 continued to cooperate with the Communists. At provincial and communal levels Socialists abandoned many alliances with the Communists in favor of coalitions with the Christian Democrats. Nevertheless, a minority of local governments, particularly in the Red Belt regions of Emilia-Romagna, Tuscany, and

Umbria, continued to be based on Communist-Socialist collaboration.

It was at the trade union level, however, that the effort to isolate the PCI failed miserably. Almost all the Socialist trade unionists, both leaders and rank-and-file members, remained in the Communist-dominated CGIL. In social, cultural, professional, and student groups Socialists usually found it easier to get along with Communists than with Catholics. The center-left, consequently, failed to push the Communists into the cold.

Socialist participation in the government produced little visible change in foreign policy. There was much talk about a moral obligation to the underdeveloped countries of the Third World, but it remained merely talk. Italian contributions to Third World economic development were, and still are, the smallest in proportion to gross national product of any advanced modern country. There was no reason that the fact should have been otherwise, given the priority of the claim of the underdeveloped parts of Italy. Both public and private businesses in Italy continued to search for new export markets and for more sources of raw materials and foodstuffs, to say nothing of additional contracts to build roads, dams, factories, pipe lines, etc. This search, of course, was independent of the nature of the coalition running the government.

The Socialists abandoned whatever earlier reservations they had had about the European Economic Community, but Italian participation in the EEC remained essentially passive, limited to weak efforts at protecting national interests. The Common Agricultural Policy of the EEC developed in the 1960s imposed a high price on Italian agriculture and consumers, for the center-left coalition defended Italy's interests ineffectively. Rhetoric about promoting further regional integration did little to counteract the nationalist involution of the EEC brought about by French President Charles de Gaulle. The Italians did resist resolutely the French efforts to turn Western Europe against the United States and NATO. Along with the West Germans they insisted upon the compatibility of the two alliances,[1] and there is little doubt that if they had ever been forced to a showdown, they would have chosen the Atlantic link over the European one. Hostility to the United States among various Italian opinion leaders because of the Vietnam war made it difficult for center-left governments to be conspicuously pro-United States, but in the 1960s a choice between the United States and Europe was not required. The Italian government favored British admission to the EEC, but could do nothing in the face of French vetoes. Nor could the Socialists persuade the left wing of the British Labour Party to abandon its hostility to the Common Market. Joint membership in the Socialist International was a useless lever for the PSI.

Center-left cabinets had their domestic disappointments also. Socialists in the government did not achieve effective decentralization. In the late 1960s parliament established regional planning commissions for nonexistent regional governments, but these commissions had no more success than the national programming committee had. Instead they became a focus of rivalry among the factions of the government parties, an additional occasion for patronage, and a potential power base in case the commissions should amount to something in the future. In some of the more advanced regions they produced useful studies and plans that could be stored away for later use.

The Christian Democrats were responsible for the center-left failure in the 1960s to create regional governments for the 15 regular regions. The DC demanded a guarantee that the Socialists would not form coalitions in the Red Belt with the PCI. In the face of the Socialist refusal to give this guarantee, the DC delayed fulfilling its pledge to implement regionalism. The issue would not be resolved until the next decade.

Of the three major economic reforms that the center-left attempted, national programming failed. A second was the nationalization of the electric power industry, undertaken in 1962 to induce the Socialists to enter the government. Depending on their ideological predilections, Italian economists still debate whether this was an improvement or a regression. The 1964 law providing for the gradual elimination of sharecropping was eminently successful, economically and socially. The former sharecroppers and, even more, those of their children who remained on the land, were slowly transformed into commercial farmers, who were better educated and who applied modern techniques and modern machinery to the improvement of agriculture.

The coalitions were also able to take some of the regressivity out of the Italian tax system. Italian statistics on income, on tax burdens, on tax evasion are unreliable. What appears clear, however, is that the proportion of government income derived from progressive direct taxes gradually increased while the proportion received from regressive indirect taxes decreased. The changes were minor, however; the tax system as a whole still remains substantially regressive.

Socialist participation in the successive cabinets of the period was responsible for a significant revision of secondary education. A unified lower middle school (grades six through eight) with a common curriculum was created to replace separate academic and vocational schools. Completion of this school satisfied the constitutional requirement for compulsory education to the age of 14.

The upper middle schools continued to exist as separate types: classic *liceo*, scientific *liceo*, normal school for training elementary school teachers, and commercial, vocational, and fine arts schools. The first two years of their curricula were now unified, to expose all Italian school children to a common basic curriculum until the age of 16. At this age a student could transfer from one type of school to another with essential prerequisites completed. The last two or three years in the upper middle schools (some have four, others five, years) continued to provide the differentiated offerings of the past. The selectivity process that controlled a young person's future had thereby been postponed. Instead of determining career choices at age 11, the reformed school system delayed critical decisions for five years when, presumably, they could be made on the basis of more training and maturity.

In the 1960s secondary school attendance was rising rapidly. The number of classrooms and teachers fell short of demand. Double shifts became common, teachers without credentials for tenure were hired, and the stresses on pupils, parents, and teachers grew. There is general agreement that the level of education improved for the mass of young people coming from families that had never before received much formal education. There is also general agreement that the quality of education was diluted from the standards required of educated elites of previous generations.

School expansion also took place at the beginning levels. There had been few public kindergartens and nursery schools. Almost all of those then existing were privately operated, the vast majority by the Catholic Church. Their expense limited access to the children of the well-to-do. The Socialists pushed for more public kindergartens and nursery schools to make them available to more of the preschool population and to reduce the role of the Church in the educational process. The DC moved slowly, to protect Church interests. It compromised by enlarging public opportunities and then increased government grants to Church schools so that they could expand in number. On more than one occasion the question of public funding for parochial schools brought the center-left coalitions to the verge of collapse.

In the long run the changes in the school system were the most important of the reforms effected by the center-left. The overall expansion of education was related to the economic development and modernization of the country. Quantity was stressed at the expense of quality. The declining reputation of the public schools among educated parents led them to prefer private schools. Whereas in the past the private schools had been looked upon as refuges for young people incapable of handling the rigors of the public *liceo*, they now became the choice of the families who could afford them. This reversal of judgments took place among anticlerical intellectuals of the left as well as conservatives and Catholics. Political postures were not permitted to control private adjustments to the conditions of contemporary life.

The 1960s witnessed the temporary political unification of the two principal socialist parties. With Socialists and Social Democrats partners in coalitions at national and local levels, it was natural to raise the question of reunification. Since the split in 1947 their relations more often than not had been affected by attitudes of rivalry and hostility. In 1956 the Socialist and Social Democratic leaders, Pietro Nenni and Giuseppe Saragat, had met at Pralognan to discuss reunification. The increasing divergences between the PSI and the Communists laid the premises for the conversation. Nothing was resolved at that time. Ten years later, in 1966, the process was renewed. A personal obstacle—who the leader of the united party would be—had been removed in 1964 when Saragat was elected to the presidency of the Italian republic. Programmatic and organizational obstacles were successfully negotiated this time. At a conference held between October 28 and 30, 1966, the new party was formed and named the Unified Socialist Party (PSU). PSIUP, in a number of ways more leftist than the Communists, remained outside the union.

The rank and file of the PSI and PSDI had not demanded unification. Consequently, the PSU was joined only at the top. The former Social Democrats became separate, identifiable factions within the new party, in competition with other Socialist factions for posts, power, and rewards. Social Democrats feared absorption into the larger PSI organization. This worry aggravated their personal concerns about future leadership roles. They feared a takeover, not a merger. The history of the rivalries and antagonisms since the split of 1947 could not be overcome quickly. The Social Democrats could feel that the circumstances of reunification justified their policies since 1947; the Socialists could feel proud of their historic tradition and larger organized base.

An effort to develop new programs and policies appropriate for a modern industrial society might have consolidated the new political formation. Such an effort could, perhaps, successfully attract growing numbers of young voters who had weak identifications with other political parties. The leadership of the PSU had neither the capacity nor the will to make the attempt. They produced nothing comparable to the 1959 Bad Godesberg program of the German Social Democratic Party, a program that modernized the basis of German socialism and provided that party's electoral successes in the 1960s. Instead, the Italian Socialists spent their time and effort in tactical maneuvering and personal rivalries. A party that might have challenged successfully both the Christian Democrats and the Communists never emerged.

Nevertheless the potentiality of a new and serious challenger induced the two largest parties to react in various ways. The Communists denounced the Socialists for splitting the working class, particularly in many cities where the PSU abandoned former local coalitions with the PCI. The Communists also made friendly approaches to left-wing Catholic political factions and social groups. The PCI continued to pursue its goal of avoiding isolation. The DC, worried by the prospect of growing Socialist influence, gave the PSU more patronage, instead of intensifying and accelerating the reform program. On the contrary, it sought to close its own ranks by providing places in the government and jobs in the public services to conservative Christian Democrats who had opposed the opening to the left throughout the decade. This consolidation then made the PSU leadership more suspicious of the sincerity of the DC commitment to reform.

Both the DC and the PSU were divided internally over the two major international events of the period, the Vietnam war and the Six-Day Arab-Israeli War of 1967. In each party left-wing groups were pro-North Vietnam and pro-Arab, as was the PCI. The official position of the center-left government was pro-United States and pro-Israel. These differences were used primarily for domestic political purposes; on the part of the PCI to undercut the unity of the PSU and the coalition government, in the other two major parties as maneuvering tools by the factions in their incessant struggles. Thus, Foreign Minister Fanfani expressed veiled sympathies for the Arab states with various proposals for mediation. His intrusion into the Vietnam war was more overt. The United States found his effort to arrange an Italian mediation irritating and uncomfortable. These activities served to undercut the position of Prime Minister Moro and also to lay the basis for Fanfani's 1971 campaign for the presidency of the republic. Fanfani could hope to get Communist and other anti-United States votes in support of his prospective candidacy. The backing that the United States was giving to the dictatorship of the colonels in Greece served to fan anti-United States feelings in Italy. More and more, parliamentary representatives of the majority coalition underlined the obvious fact that Italy's commitment to the Atlantic community was limited geographically to Europe and implied no support for U.S. policies beyond the Atlantic area.

To offset the anti-U.S. atmosphere President Saragat paid a state visit to the United States in September 1967, accompanied by Foreign Minister Fanfani. The traditional friendship between the two countries was reaffirmed. Presumably suggestions were made to President Lyndon B. Johnson about reducing the U.S. commitment in the war in Southeast Asia. Since Saragat was considering running for reelection, Fanfani's position was thereby defined. Saragat's pro-U.S. stance, however, made him more unpopular among the left-wing factions of his own PSU.

Strains within the PSU were matched by strains between Socialists and their Christian Democratic allies. Two major scandals found each on opposite sides of the issues. In the summer of 1965 the former minister of finance, Giuseppe Trabucchi, Christian Democrat, was charged with corruption while in office. He was accused of accepting large bribes that presumably went to his party. Since he was still a deputy, it was necessary for his accusers to get his parliamentary immunity lifted in order to bring him into court. The DC defeated this move, but found itself abandoned by its Socialist, Social Democratic, and Republican allies.

More serious was the charge made in 1967 by two Socialist journalists that General Giovanni De Lorenzo had been plotting a coup d'état in the summer of 1964. Since Antonio Segni, then president of Italy, was implicated, the Christian Democratic Party had to defend its honor. Although the courts finally exonerated De Lorenzo, certain aspects of the issue remain a mystery. Many Socialists joined the call for a parliamentary investigation of the affair, but the government refused, claiming that state secrets were involved. Here Moro was acting to defend the image of his own party for the following years's elections, and in this he succeeded. A subsequent public criticism of the two journalists by President Saragat further divided the factions in the PSU.[2]

The question of divorce added another stress to the cohesion of the governing coalition. In 1965 the Socialist deputy, Loris Fortuna, introduced a divorce bill in the Chamber of Deputies. Although it was a private member bill, the issue immediately put the DC at odds with its lay partners. The Catholic Church opposed any divorce bill absolutely, no matter how stringent its provisions, and the DC had no option but to defend the Church's position. The issue thereby became one of party, drawn out for years before it was resolved.

In this climate the country went into the 1968 parliamentary election on May 19 and 20. The DC gained slightly; in the Chamber of Deputies its proportion rose from 38.3 percent of the total vote to 39.1 percent. The conservative parties, Liberal, Monarchist, and Missini, all declined. PSIUP received 4.5 percent, retaining 23 of its 24 Chamber seats. The big gainer was the PCI, which increased from 25.3 to 26.9 percent of the electorate and received 11 more seats in the Chamber. The big loser was the PSU. It lost almost 25 percent of the vote that the PSI and PSDI together had totaled in 1963. Part of their former voters went over to PSIUP, but it was obvious that another part had gone to the Communists and, in small measure, to the DC[3] (see Table 3.1).

Moro and his party could be pleased with the outcome. They had reassured their moderate electorate that there was no danger from the alliance with the Socialists. They had recouped part of their 1963 losses to the Liberals. The PSU no longer loomed as a possible threat to their leading position. What the DC had failed to do was to block the continued advance of the Communists. The PCI received the largest vote in its history to that point. Analysis of the election results indicated that it was making headway, especially among the young voters, which augured well for the party's future. The PCI had staved off the attempt to isolate it and to steal its electorate.

Inside the PSU the atmosphere was bitter. Erstwhile Social Democrats and former PSI leaders could agree that the basic cause of their electoral defeat was their failure to achieve significant reforms. They could agree on little else, however, and mutual recriminations increased. The PSU had been only partially unified at best; the election returns brought the unification process to a halt. Many Socialists blamed Moro and his strategy of delay for their failure. Others, however, believed Moro to be sincere in his commitment to reform, recognizing that he could not move too far ahead of his own traditional electorate. The latter Socialist group, led by Nenni, felt that Moro had to be supported in the effort to reorganize a new center-left coalition, since there was still a good majority in parliament. The alternative would be a return to weak center-right governments like those of the 1950s, with the Socialists again in opposition. Neither the country nor the Socialists would benefit. Within the Socialists, Moro's enemies won out, arguing that the PSU would have to remain outside the government while it reassessed its position. On May 31, 1968, the Central Committee of the PSU voted to cut its ties to the center-left coalition. The era of the Moro-Nenni-Saragat triumvirate had ended.

Three weeks later Giovanni Leone, speaker of the Chamber of Deputies, formed a one-party DC minority cabinet as a caretaker for

TABLE 3.1: Results of Four Elections to the Italian Chamber of Deputies, 1968-79

Parties*	May 9, 1968 Valid Votes Number	Percent	Seats	May 7, 1972 Valid Votes Number	Percent	Seats	June 20, 1976 Valid Votes Number	Percent	Seats	June 3, 1979 Valid Votes Number	Percent	Seats
Christian Democrat (DC)	12,441,553	39.1	266	12,919,270	38.7	266	14,209,519	38.7	262	14,007,594	38.3	262
Communist (PCI)	8,557,404	26.9	177	9,072,454	27.1	179	12,614,650	34.4	228	11,107,883	30.4	201
Unified Socialist (PSU)	4,605,832	14.5	91	—	—	—	—	—	—	—	—	—
Socialist (PSI)	—	—	—	3,210,427	9.6	61	3,540,309	9.6	57	3,586,256	9.8	62
Italian Social Movement (MSI)	1,414,794	4.5	24	2,896,762	8.7	56	2,238,339	6.1	35	1,924,251	5.3	30
Social Democrat (PSDI)	—	—	—	1,717,539	5.1	29	1,239,492	3.4	15	1,403,873	3.8	20
Republican (PRI)	626,567	2.0	9	954,597	2.9	15	1,135,546	3.1	14	1,106,766	3.0	16
Socialist Party of Proletarian Unity (PSIUP)	1,414,544	4.4	23	648,763	1.9	—	—	—	—	—	—	—
Proletarian Democracy (DP)	—	—	—	—	—	—	557,025	1.5	6	501,431	1.4	6
Liberal (PLI)	1,851,060	5.8	31	1,297,105	3.9	20	480,122	1.3	5	708,022	1.9	9
Monarchist (PDIUM)	414,423	1.3	6	—	—	—	—	—	—	—	—	—
Radical (PR)	—	—	—	—	—	—	394,439	1.1	4	1,259,362	3.4	18

*In addition, local ethnic and linguistic parties have a few deputies.

Sources: Istituto Centrale di Statistica, *Annuario Statistico Italiano 1977* (Rome: Published by the Institute, 1977), p. 100; *Annuario Statistico Italiano 1979*, p. 94.

the summer holidays, while the Socialists were deciding what to do. A PSU party congress called in October to resolve the issue of participation was divided into five factions. Two of them, originally Social Democratic for the most part, plus some former PSI autonomists led by Nenni, succeeded in getting 51 percent of the votes at the congress. Included in this group was Antonio Mancini, leader of the Socialist organization in Calabria. The group gained temporary control of the party organization, further irritating many of the former PSI wing. The internal equilibrium of the PSU was precarious.

Provisionally almost all of the factions agreed that they had no choice but to continue the coalition. The exception was the small Riccardo Lombardi group, hostile to the center-left since 1963. As a result the Leone government resigned on November 19. In less than a month the Christian Democrat, Mariano Rumor, formed a new cabinet. All the principal PSU leaders participated in the government in a move designed to hold the party together.

The new government reformed the pension system, but accomplished little else because renewed strife erupted inside the PSU in the spring of 1969. Involved were policy issues such as bringing the Communists, who were themselves evolving rapidly, into the center-left. Another dispute concerned the role of the police in an atmosphere of increasing violence. But personal rivalries and fears were more important. Saragat hoped to obtain reelection in 1971, but found many PSU leaders hostile. Ministers from PSI factions envisioned a future Socialist prime minister and were willing to compensate the DC by giving it the presidency of the republic. They knew that Fanfani had his eye on the post and thought he might be willing to support a Socialist candidate for prime minister. In this climate Mancini and his followers shifted to an alliance with Francesco De Martino, leader of those Socialists hostile to the Social Democrats. The Social Democrats felt their position threatened both in the government and inside the PSU. Efforts to mediate between the contenders failed. On July 3, 1969, the party split. The Socialists resurrected their old title, PSI. De Martino became secretary-general of the party. The Social Democrats continued using the PSU label for a while and then returned to their traditional PSDI label.[4]

Some of those who went over to the PSDI had come from the old PSI. Others originally from the PSDI now entered the PSI. Leading trade unionists, chief of whom was Italo Viglianesi, secretary-general of the UIL, joined the PSI. The loss of much of their trade union component isolated the Social Democrats even more from the organized workers' movement.

The reunification of Italian socialism had lasted fewer than three years. Unlike Christian Democrats and Communists, the Socialists were incapable of maintaining that minimum of unity in diversity necessary to keep a large party together in the complexity of modern Italy. The policy issues over which disagreement existed do not appear sufficiently serious to explain the rupture. Instead, the personal ambitions and animosities of leaders, the maneuverings of factions, and the distribution of patronage played the significant roles. As a result, a strong third force between Catholicism and communism failed to emerge.

NOTES

1. Primo Vannicelli, *Italy, NATO, and the European Community: The Interplay of Foreign Policy and Domestic Politics* (Cambridge: Harvard University, Center for International Affairs, 1974), pp. 47-51.

2. Giorgio Galli, *Storia della Democrazia Cristiana* (Bari: Laterza, 1978), pp. 280-81.

3. Giuseppe Mammarella, *L'Italia dalla caduta del fascismo ad oggi* (Bologna: Il Mulino, 1978), pp. 426-27.

4. Giuseppe Tamburrano, *Storia e cronaca del centro sinistra* (Milano: Feltrinelli, 1973).

4

THE EVOLUTION
OF THE COMMUNISTS

In the early 1960s the PCI had already endorsed reformism, as a method, if not as a goal. Palmiro Togliatti had wondered publicly if the class struggle, in its orthodox Marxist version, made sense in the modern developed countries. Asserting openly that if it came to power it would respect parliamentary democracy and a multiparty system, the party then qualified such affirmations in a number of ways. It insisted it was still a revolutionary party because the ultimate goal was the transformation of society, even though this transformation was to be achieved gradually over a substantial period of time by democratic means. Italian communism was not interested merely in making the welfare capitalist state work better, which it claimed the social democrats of the Western world had settled for. It limited its acceptance of the multiparty system to those parties seeking socialist goals. The PCI continued to preach the hegemony of the working class, a concept initiated by its patron saint, Antonio Gramsci. This was supposed to be different from the dictatorship of the proletariat, but nobody, including Communists, could agree on just what it meant.

On one criterion there was clear agreement: the internal unity and cohesion of the party must be maintained. The organizational principle of democratic centralism was not to be challenged. Debate and discussion were to be promoted, but organized groups and factions were still proscribed. Giorgio Amendola, a leading Communist, had suggested the possibility of majority and minority votes within party decision-making organizations, but the suggestion was dropped. Nor was there any noticeable sentiment for cutting the ties to the international communist movement, as the Yugoslavs had

39

done in 1948 and the Chinese after 1960. These ties were not those of subordination to Moscow, for as early as 1957 Togliatti had made it clear that the Communist Party of the Soviet Union was no longer the guiding party for the international movement. But the continuation of symbolic and probably financial links distinguished the PCI from even left-wing socialist parties, in Italy and elsewhere. The PCI, in other words, remained a party "different from the others."

In the middle 1960s the major foreign relations problem of the PCI was the Soviet-Chinese rivalry within the international movement. The Italian Party was caught between two fires. On the one hand it challenged the Soviet Party's effort to excommunicate the Chinese. Since it was defending the right of Italians to determine their own path to socialism it had to endorse a similar right for the Chinese, even though formal contacts with the Chinese Party were practically nonexistent. On the other hand, the Chinese way, at least at the verbal level, was an extremist revolutionary one, at the opposite pole from the reformist procedures advocated by the Italians. As a result the PCI found itself on the receiving end of a barrage of Chinese attacks and insults, denounced as revisionist and an enemy of the true revolutionary spirit. The outbreak of the cultural revolution in China in 1967 aggravated tensions. Nevertheless, the PCI continued to object to all efforts by the Soviets to call a world conference of Communist parties to read the Chinese out of the international movement. Together with the Romanian and a few other Communist parties, it blocked such Soviet efforts in 1968 and 1969. The PCI was aware that what could be done to China might, in the future, be done to it.[1] Only ten years later, in 1978, a different Chinese Communist government made an initial opening to the Italians for the reestablishment of normal relations. In 1979, after the visit of the Chinese president, Hua Kuo Feng, to Rome at the end of a European tour, the premises were laid for a resumption of regular contacts between the two parties. The Italians insisted that such a resumption excluded any obligation to endorse the Chinese position of intense hostility to the Soviet Union.

In Italian foreign policy affairs the PCI maintained its already established positions. It had publicly endorsed Italy's membership in the European Economic Community in 1962, reversing its negative vote of 1957. This shift did not gain the PCI one of its ambitions, immediate membership in the Italian delegation to the European Parliament at Strasburg. Part of the price it demanded in December 1964 for supporting Saragat's successful candidacy for president of the republic was participation in the Italian delegation. The Italian parliament, not the president, chose the delegation, however, and the most Saragat could do was to use his influence in his party and its allies. This took time, so that it was not until 1969 that a PCI group, led by Giorgio Amendola, was included in the Italian contingent.

Italy's other major foreign policy commitment, membership in NATO, continued to be the object of PCI hostility. The Communists could do nothing but denounce the alliance, so they did that vigorously, repeating their slogan "Italy out of NATO and NATO out of Italy." As the United States got mired down in the Vietnam war after 1965, the Communists were able to use the war to mobilize numerous anti-U.S. demonstrations and to involve non-Communists in their anti-U.S. campaign. This was one more technique of escaping the isolation that the center-left policies of the time were supposed to achieve.

For the Communists, as for the other Italian parties, foreign policy was a tool of domestic politics, and their domestic relationships primarily concerned the Catholic and Socialist camps. Pope John XXIII and Vatican Council II had created ferment in the Catholic world, even within traditionalist Italian Catholicism. As the Pope extended his hands to non-Catholics and to nonbelievers, they were obliged to respond and, if possible, to understand him. Since Togliatti had always tried to moderate the inherent anticlericalism and anti-Catholicism of the Italian left, the Pope's policies stimulated him to a renewed effort. In 1964 Togliatti urged his party to recognize that a religious faith can stimulate aspirations for a Socialist society. In his Yalta memorial to Khrushchev that year, he called on the international movement to recognize the contribution the forces of religion and the Church could make to the cause of the working class.

Most members of the PCI were and are anticlerical and antireligious. For them relations with the Catholic world could be at best an arrangement—not even a marriage—of convenience. In the mid sixties a leading Communist, Pietro Ingrao, argued that efforts should be made to promote such arrangements with the left-wing anticapitalist elements of the Catholic world and of the DC. It was of little importance whether their anticapitalist views originated from a corporativist or from a social Christian tradition. Amendola, arguing a contrary line, advocated reaching out to the Socialist and even Social Democratic camp instead of the Catholic one. In 1964 Amendola asserted that traditionally conceived communism had failed in the Western world. What was needed, therefore, was a new party of the working class, neither Communist nor Social Democratic. The outlines of this new party were vague. The goal was socialist democracy, but what that meant in the way of concrete policies and organizational arrangements was unclear.

For two years the debate between these two strategies divided the PCI leadership. The political forces to which the strategies were directed remained suspicious, when not hostile. The Catholics found it difficult to take at face value the PCI abandonment of hostility toward religion just as many Socialists found it hard to believe in the PCI conversion to socialist democracy. Both strategies were part of the general Communist policy of avoiding isolation. Ingrao's was the safer for his party in that it did not propose more than a deal between political powers, each of which would be able to preserve its nature and identity. Amendola's was the riskier for it would require all partners to abandon historic natures and identities, to create something new and untried. In the end neither strategy prevailed; the debate petered out as elements of each position were fitted into the continuing process of adjustment to the center-left in Italy and to the larger European world beyond the frontiers.

Luigi Longo, secretary-general of the PCI after Togliatti's death, continued the trends set in motion by his predecessor. In reaching out to the Catholic world he asserted at the Eleventh Party Congress in 1966, "Just as we are against the confessional state, so are we against state atheism. And is it not possible, is it not necessary to seek together points of agreement and of collaboration so that we may succeed in building together a new society?"[2] In reaching out to and beyond Socialists and Social Democrats in 1968, the party leaders insisted that their long-run strategic objective was socialist democracy, to be achieved through the union of all working and democratic forces, secular and Catholic, with a plurality of parties, organizations, and social groupings. The following year at the Twelfth Party Congress, Longo described his party's goal as:

> . . . a socialist society rich in democratic articulations, based on a popular consensus, on the direct and active participation of the masses, on the laic, nonideological character of the state. An objective, that is, of a socialist society, decentralized, nonbureaucratic, in which religious liberty, the freedom of culture, of science and of art, the freedom of information, of expression and circulation of ideas. [We] will make socialism in Italy, with the presence of a plurality of parties and social organizations committed to a free and democratic dialectic of differing positions, something qualitatively different from the experiences hitherto known and fully corresponding to the traditions and the will of our people.[3]

This claim to the inheritance of the bourgeois democratic revolutions of the eighteenth and nineteenth centuries was made by a party still calling itself Marxist-Leninist. That the inheritance corresponded to the traditions of the Italian people was debatable, for those traditions could as easily be described as authoritarian, dogmatic, and oligarchical. Indeed, the Communist Party still exhibited these characteristics along with other Italian political parties and social and religious organizations. The claim was, nevertheless, a recognition of changing social and cultural conditions and of the appeal of democratic symbols to growing numbers of Italians who were benefiting from the modernization and secularization of Italian society. Blue-collar workers and alienated intellectuals were the traditional groups in European society to whom Marxism had made its appeal; in Italy landless farm laborers and sharecroppers had also responded. Now the peasants' share of the labor force was shrinking rapidly. The number of blue-collar workers in industry had peaked in the middle 1960s and then began a slow decline. The middle classes had always been relatively numerous in twentieth-century Italy so that after World War II Togliatti had excluded small owners, artisans, white-collar employees, and professionals from the ranks of the class enemy. In the middle 1960s the number of small and middle-sized firms was increasing so that the PCI found it beneficial to enlarge its appeal to include their owners and managers. The class enemy was now further limited to the small number of large private monopolists. Since a substantial and growing number of the large firms were publicly controlled, this left very few enemies in principle. The evolution of doctrinal positions, the open acceptance of the legal and political tradition of the bourgeois revolutions, was linked in part to the policy of expanding Communist penetration into the growing instead of the shrinking sectors of Italian society.

This penetration did not increase party membership. During the middle and late 1960s the number of party cardholders remained relatively stable at approximately 1.6 million. The social composition of party members gradually changed, however, partly as the result of the normal processes of aging and death and partly as a result of the upgrading of the educational levels and skills of the Italian people. An increasing share of the membership, particularly of the activists, came from the middle class.

The gradual growth in the size of the PCI electorate was demonstrated in the 1968 parliamentary election. The 1.6 percent increase in its popular vote for the Chamber of Deputies resulting in the addition of 11 seats in the Chamber indicated that the center-left had failed to erode the PCI's constituency. The Communists' gain among young voters roughly equaled the attractiveness of the DC to the youth cohorts. The Communists held their traditional constituency, even that part of it opposed to the recent developments in party doctrine, and at the same time they gained ground in sectors of society hitherto suspicious of the party's objectives.

In the 1960s these suspicions had hardly disappeared. In spite of the claims Communists made for the Italian way to socialism, disbelief in their claims was based on a variety of fears about the real nature of the PCI:

a) it is the enemy of religion;
b) it is not committed to the rules of representative democracy, no matter what it says about the democratic way to socialism;
c) it is the agent of a foreign power (the Soviet Union);
d) it is ready to use violence to gain its ends;
e) its internal cohesion and discipline (democratic centralism) is dangerous to the country;
f) it is the enemy of private property.[4]

The changes in Communist doctrine were the result of many considerations: not only judgments about the direction of events in Italy and the Western world and disappointments over developments in Eastern Europe and in East Asia, but also an attempt to meet and to allay the suspicions that so much of the Italian electorate felt toward the PCI. The slowness of the increase in the Communist vote indicated that for many people those fears were still alive.

Events in Czechoslovakia in early 1968 were momentous for the Italian Communist Party. The victory of the party group led by Alexander Dubcek opened the way in Czechoslovakia for a new set of policies that were later labeled "Communism with a human face." The orthodox command economy was abandoned for a socialist market economy. Censorship was loosened, public dissent permitted, and the role of the political police restricted. As successive reforms were instituted during the "Prague Spring," the outside world had the chance to see that there were certain Communists who had different perceptions of the meaning of their doctrines.

Not surprisingly important leadership groups and other intellectuals within the PCI quickly developed a strong emotional commitment to the success of the Prague experiment. Czech Communists were natural allies for the PCI in the international Communist movement. Their example indicated a path that other fraternal parties might take. They provided a way to show skeptics that liberal principles were not merely false propaganda put out by Communists seeking power but were taken seriously by Communists who were in power.

The PCI was seriously shocked in August 1968 by the Soviet-led invasion of Czechoslovakia. Not only did the executive bureau of the PCI criticize the Soviet Union openly but it also did not withdraw the criticism despite the protests of many local and sectional leaders of the party who were still emotionally identified with Russia. In 1956 the PCI had rationalized the Soviet invasion of Hungary. In 1968 it rejected the Soviet justification of its attack on an ally, just as it later rejected the Brezhnev Doctrine, with its assertion of the right to intervene in the internal affairs of the countries of the socialist world.

The negative reaction in Italy to the invasion of Czechoslovakia was widespread throughout all sectors of the political world. President Saragat and the Christian Democratic cabinet condemned the Warsaw Pact outright. The Chamber of Deputies did likewise in a special session of August 29. The PCI, after the initial criticism of Soviet behavior, moderated and differentiated its position from the other parties by blaming all the trouble on the policy of military blocs to which Italy contributed with its membership in NATO. Some of its leaders thought the party had gone too far in its initial reaction. They worried about their relations with the Soviet Union in the international Communist movement. Furthermore, they had second thoughts about the importance of the myth of the Soviet Union to the party rank and file, the myth of the Communist fatherland as the bulwark of international socialism.

Nevertheless, the destruction of communism with a human face in Czechoslovakia, coupled with the enunciation of the Brezhnev Doctrine, created obvious potential dangers for the future of the PCI. On paper the Italian way to socialism was more liberal and deviant than anything produced during the Prague Spring. If Dubcek's reforms were intolerable to the Warsaw Pact countries, what could a future democratic socialism in Italy face? Was such a regime possible in a Europe dominated by the Soviet Union?

August 1968, therefore, led the Italian Communists to a reappraisal of the international situation in Europe and the larger Western world. For almost twenty years the PCI had opposed NATO and Italy's membership in the alliance. Now NATO was seen to have virtues formerly unperceived. The shift in perception was gradual. Years of opposition to the alliance had to be overcome. Internal resistance had to be persuaded. The Vietnam war was still being waged full force with all the anti-U.S. hostilities it produced in Italy and elsewhere. Nevertheless, the process of reevaluation had begun. In the usual pattern it moved slowly. In 1969 the NATO treaty came up for renewal, as its own terms provided. The Christian Democratic-led government renewed it with little hesitation. The Communists still formally opposed renewal. Although a few elaborate articles were written by Communist intellectuals in criticism of the pact, no major campaign was organized, no enormous propaganda effort was launched against the government's foreign policy. A start had been made.

NOTES

1. Donald L. M. Blackmer, *Unity in Diversity: Italian Communism and the Communist World* (Cambridge: M.I.T. Press, 1968).

2. Quoted in *Il Crociato*, February 2, 1966.

3. See resolutions of the executive bureau of the PCI of July 17, 1968, and the speech of Longo to the Twelfth Congress of the PCI, 1969. Reprinted in *Almanacco PCI '76*, pp. 251-52.

4. Giacomo Sani, "Mass Level Constraints on Political Realignments: Perception of Anti-System Parties in Italy," *British Journal of Political Science*, January 1976, pp. 1-31.

5

THE CHANGING
SOCIAL CLIMATE

The years between 1968 and 1970 mark a turning point in postwar Italian history. The series of center-left coalitions, a relatively stable political formula, was breaking down because of the Socialist electoral losses of 1968 and the split of the PSU in 1969. The PSI was now torn between perpetuation of the formula and a return to association with the Communists, a return made more attractive by the evolution of the PCI. Two decades of continuous economic growth were coming to an end. External markets that had been a major stimulus to this growth were changing their character. Now foreign competition and growing protectionism started to challenge Italian sales expansion. At the same time world prices of raw materials and foodstuffs, upon which Italy was increasingly dependent, began to rise steadily, bringing about a slow deterioration in Italy's terms of trade.

These political and economic developments were not immediately critical. What struck Italy with full force, instead, was a social explosion initiated in the universities that then spread to other parts of society. The student movement erupted in early 1968. The May revolt in the Parisian universities stimulated the Italian students further, although in no single week did the violence in Italy equal the intensity of May Week in France. Behind the surge of drama and excitement lay growing academic frustrations, national disappointments, and international myths. Together they produced an outburst of Catholic and Marxist utopianism that temporarily swept the universities and quickly spread to the senior secondary schools. The foci of the movement were in the huge urban universities of central and northern Italy: Rome, Turin, Milan, and Padua. The smaller provincial universities, though not immune, were less vulnerable.

For several years young Italians had been affected by international mythologies, particularly those of the Third World revolutions. The Cuban revolution and the figures of Fidel Castro and Che Guevara; the cultural revolution in China and the figures of Mao Tse-tung and Lin Piao; the Vietnamese war of the North against the South and against United States intervention, a struggle led by Ho Chi Minh—all provided mythologies and charismatic heroes to stir youthful imaginations. Closer to home the Prague Spring with its hopes and final delusions was an additional stimulant. The civil rights movement and anti-Vietnam war campaigns in United States universities set further examples. Unlike U.S. students, however, the Italians faced neither a race problem nor a wartime military draft. In the heated utopian atmosphere the distance of the myths made them more attractive. The Frankfurt school of social thought, particularly Herbert Marcuse's amalgam of Marxism and Freudianism, provided an explanation of the despised modern industrial world that made the serious study of Marx, Freud, or that world unnecessary.

The student movement initially contended with issues that were much more immediate. The inadequacies of the Italian university system were all too visible. An unexpectedly rapid increase in the numbers of students between 1964 and 1968 exposed the faculties and the inadequate facilities to tremendous pressures. Many students found it impossible to attend courses in the overcrowded buildings and classrooms. There were far too few teachers. Medicine, law, architecture, the social sciences, and the humanities bore the brunt of the expanded enrollments. The physical and biological sciences, engineering, and agriculture were less crowded. The large urban universities suffered more than the provincial ones. Antiquated curricula and autocratic academicism—anachronistic approaches and illogical requirements—aggravated the problems created by huge numbers.

Many students experienced financial difficulties and were concerned that the degree they hoped to acquire would have questionable value after graduation. The shift in values and manners and the enlarged gap between the students and their parents made the younger generation more dependent on each other for reference groups and role models.

The attack on the universities was physical as well as moral. Classes were disrupted. Professors could not teach. Buildings were vandalized and sometimes wrecked. Contrary to the ancient Italian tradition that university precincts were beyond the normal jurisdiction of the regular authorities, the police were brought in to restore order. Some universities were closed for months at a time. Activist students made sporadic attempts to create counter-courses or counter-universities. Academic standards were denounced. The examination of individual students was rejected in favor of group examinations with the same grades for all. Everybody was to pass because discrimination on the basis of traditional criteria was intolerable. The right to enroll automatically included the right to graduate. Professors were sometimes threatened with death if a student was failed. Most of these demands did not survive the tense years between 1968 and 1970. Outside the university the suspicion of the quality of the degrees conferred after 1968 worked against the graduates.

It became apparent that the student movement could do little to change the university immediately, so the students shifted their attack to society at large. The activists concluded that the university was simply a functional agent of the power elites dominating Italy and the world: a machine producing graduates as replacement parts to fit into the slots assigned by the establishment to solidify and perpetuate the status quo. That the Italian universities, like other university systems of the Western world, traditionally and currently performed the role of critic and opponent of established ideas and institutions went unrecognized by the student movement. The activists replaced their goal of reforming the higher educational system with their ambition to achieve the revolutionary overthrow of industrial society, its values, its economic and political orders.

Student activists saw society's supreme value as consumerism; the rejection of the consumer society became their major theme. In the name of a higher liberty and of greater equality they also attacked the constituted powers, the judicial order, and the family. Throughout the country's history most Italians had never been fortunate enough to participate in a consumer society; the change in their condition was very recent and far from complete.

Large numbers of students did not follow the activists in the shift of the attack from the university to the overthrow of the social order. Inside the university the pressures to conform to the latest activist fashion, the fear of being ostracized by their peers, led them to participate in the movement, whatever their doubts. It was part of being modern and being young, and the youth cult was an important part of the myth (as it had been for futurism and fascism). The external aspects of the youth movement were the easiest to assimilate and many students became prisoners of the latest fads in personal life style and mass culture. Abandoning the universities to agitate in factories was something else, however; and only the most militant went out to challenge the larger world.

The utopianism of the student movement had both positive and negative aspects. The extraordinary, if short lived, confidence of the student revolt was based on the optimism of a generation that had never personally known world wars or great depressions. In the lifetime of these students much had changed and much greater change appeared feasible. The positive consequences of decisive action were taken for granted. On the other hand, the movement had no thoughtful and articulated ideal model to replace detested reality, no strategy of action and no organization. Student action deteriorated into interminable debates in assemblies. No authority to make decisions was granted to any one person or group. Only the entire assembly could decide. Incapable of distinguishing between authoritarianism and authority, the assemblies after a time split into rival groups that directed most of their energies against each other. All the activists considered themselves to be to the left, whatever their spiritual or ideological origins. As they fractured into splinter groups the confusion of political identities increased. One group at the University of Rome took the name of Nazi-Maoist. As the clashes among them grew, some groups would be identified as neo-Fascist, others as Communists of various leanings.[1]

In the general confusion one thing was clear. The traditional parties with their regular youth groups had lost all control of organized student life. The Catholic, Communist, Socialist, and other youth organizations were all pushed aside for the time being because of their links to the defenders of the status quo. Students who had a Catholic Action tradition from secondary school, university, or Catholic workers organizations found their original spiritual home intolerable. The ferment in Catholic life spurred by Pope John XXIII and Vatican Council II was soon considered anachronistic and insufficient. The Christian Democratic Party, hesitating over even limited reforms, was rejected. Some of the future leaders of terrorist organizations had strong Catholic institutional origins. Renato Curcio, founder of the Red Brigades, had attended the Catholic Higher School of Sociological Studies at Trento. Antonio Negri, who later became the key intellectual theorist of terrorist activity, emerged from the left wing of the Catholic Federation of University Students.

Marxist students, Socialist and Communist, similarly repudiated their original political homes. As the PSI entered the center-left coalitions with bourgeois parties, as it united with the PSDI between 1966 and 1969, young Socialists who considered these moves a betrayal of the Socialist tradition might find a home in PSIUP or move out of Socialist party organizations completely. Likewise, young Communists could feel that the evolution of their party in the 1960s had culminated in its complete abandonment of revolutionary goals. The constant denunciation of the PCI as revisionist by the Chinese Communists reinforced this belief.

The Communist movement had always had critics to its left, outside and inside the party, who strongly opposed the strategy pursued by Togliatti in the postwar years. Whether they were labeled Bordigaists, after Amedeo Bordiga, the first secretary of the party in 1921, or Trotskyites, their numbers were insignificant and their impact marginal. In the early 1960s domestic and international developments stimulated new critical groups who elaborated their own reinterpretations of Marxism. They went back to the pre-1848 Marx of the philosophical manuscripts and the German ideology to emphasize his humanism rather than his scientific and economic determinism. Marx's ideas of alienation fascinated them for they were in the mood to feel alienated. These young ex-PCI and ex-PSI intellectuals founded and published new reviews with small circulations but much verve. Such publications as *Quaderni Rossi, Classe operaia, Giovane critica, Quaderni Piacentini* treated themes and issues that later formed some of the ideas of the student movement and young trade union extremists. From them came the suggestions for counter-universities, for an alternative culture. From them came the shift to the attack on the larger society, for these groups were a decade ahead of the students.[2] Some of them organized the Communist Party of Italy (Marxist-Leninist), which was suspected of receiving Chinese money.

The ferment outside the PCI had its counterpart within the party. A minority of regular party members, including some parliamentarians and members of the Central Committee such as Rossana Rossanda, Lucio Magri, Luigi Pintor, and Aldo Natoli, had protested their party's strategy and what they considered its excessive opportunism. Infected by the currents circulating in the political atmosphere, opposed to the policies of gradualism and their party's opening to non-Marxist social groups, they advocated a return to a revolutionary strategy and the traditional emphasis on the proletariat. Their dissidence became increasingly open, the wider party membership was made aware of their criticism, and they began to take on the characteristics of a faction. In early 1969 they published a new review, *Manifesto*, in which they proposed a line admittedly close to that of the Chinese Communist Party. They denied any official relations with that party, however, and repudiated suspicions of Chinese financial support. The new publication brought the conflict to a head. Charged by the top party leadership with the Leninist sin of fractionalism, the dissidents were expelled from the PCI in the middle of 1969. They would later organize a small party named Manifesto, which became one of the more prominent groups of the extra-parliamentary left—those groups outside parliamentary politics and contemptuous of it.

Some of the leaders of the student movement entered the new party; some joined the groups associated with the little magazines. The action was shifting away from the schools. By 1970 the student movement was dying as a nationwide phenomenon, although student discontent continued in a variety of forms. Its one lasting impact on higher education was a change of admission policies legislated in 1970. All requirements for admission to specific faculties were eliminated.* Any graduate of any five-year senior high school could enter any faculty of any state university. Since Italian universities are not liberal arts colleges,† but rather professional schools, this change meant that the universities were flooded with students unprepared for the courses of study they were selecting. Together with the continuing expansion of enrollments in the 1970s, only slightly relieved by the creation of new universities and the addition of new faculties to already existing institutions, the problems of Italian higher education became even more unmanageable than before.

The excitement of these years stimulated changes in the position of women. They had received the vote in 1946. The 1948 constitution provided for the equality of the sexes. The historic Latin tradition of male domination of public life, however, had left little scope for women outside the roles of wife and mother, the protector of the family and the home. Peasant women had labored in the fields for centuries, but only gradually had certain social roles outside the family become acceptable. Early in the twentieth century professions such as nursing and teaching, particularly at the elementary level, had become standard women's fields. The beginnings of the industrial revolution before World War I brought women into the factories in small numbers, especially in the textile industry. As in other countries women moved into office work, or into shopkeeping, to supplement their traditional jobs as seamstresses and dressmakers. As late as the 1950s women received, on the whole, less formal education than men and even in the 1960s there were far fewer females than males among the increasing numbers of university students.

---

*A faculty of an Italian university is the counterpart of a school or college of a U.S. university. For example, Italians refer to the Faculty of Law of the University of Rome.

†The liberal arts preparation is offered in the classic and scientific *licei*.

A small number of women had been active in cultural and public life since the late nineteenth century but their ranks grew slowly. It took years to implement the formal emancipation embodied in the republican constitution. The accumulated corpus of legislation and court decisions that discriminated against women had to be replaced piecemeal. In the 1960s these efforts started to bear fruit. Women began to appear in greater numbers at the directive levels of the state bureaucracy, to receive appointments to the judiciary, and later to the diplomatic service. At the upper levels of politics they remained few. A small number had been elected to the parliament of 1948, but in subsequent elections their numbers shrank. The first woman cabinet minister, Tina Anselmi, was not appointed until 1976.

Secularization and modernization of Italian society accelerated in the 1960s. The impact of Pope John XXIII and Vatican Council II was evident even though no new doctrines specifically changing the position of women in the Church or society were promulgated. Italian women, traditionally responsive to ecclesiastical influence, were moving away from clerical control, particularly the younger generations. The election patterns of 1963 and 1968 were one indication. The growing ferment over woman's role in the family, and the question of the indissolubility of the family, was another. In the latter part of the 1960s, public policy on the family was fought out over the issue of divorce.

The struggle began in 1965 when the Socialist deputy Loris Fortuna introduced a divorce bill in the Chamber of Deputies. It was a private member bill, rather than a party one, for these were the years of the center-left coalitions, and the PSI was cautious about upsetting its relations with its Christian Democratic ally. Other lay parties were equally careful for similar reasons. The Communists were chary on two grounds. If they pushed the divorce issue their strategy of making contacts with the Catholic world, of engaging in dialogue with Catholic intellectuals, of attempting to allay the fears of the Church hierarchy about future Communist intentions, would be undercut. In addition a large part of the rank-and-file party membership, the electoral sympathizers, as distinct from party activists and intellectuals, were quite traditionalist in social perspectives and personal morality. Opinion polls taken at the time indicated that a majority of the public, especially of the women, opposed divorce. As a result the Fortuna bill made little initial headway.

Throughout the postwar period the political parties had always had women's affiliates that were expected to deal with women's issues and to function as informational and electoral agencies for their party sponsors. Like similar groups elsewhere they spoke mainly to the already converted. Taking their cues from the parties that supported them, they also treated the divorce issue with caution. They too were aware of the findings of the public opinion polls. When the currents released by the student movement and the extra-parliamentary groups began to sweep Italy in the late 1960s, the women's political associations were unprepared, just as the party youth organizations had been caught short. They found themselves outflanked by a small but growing and aggressive feminist movement, independent of political party ties.

The changed atmosphere brought the Fortuna bill back to life. Antonio Baslini of the Liberal Party became an additional formal sponsor in 1968. All the lay parties rallied behind the bill. The Christian Democrats led the government but, except for the support of the Monarchists and neo-Fascist Missini, they now found themselves isolated in their opposition to divorce. The Catholic Church, cautious since the days of Pope John XXIII about openly intervening in Italian politics, mounted a public campaign to oppose the bill. The Church called it unconstitutional, a violation of Article 7, which incorporated the Lateran Accords of 1929 into the constitution. In 1967 the parliamentary Committee on Constitutional Affairs had decided that the divorce bill would not require an amendment to the constitution. In 1970 this judgment was upheld in a decision of the Constitutional Court. To make the bill more palatable to the Catholic community, amendments were inserted to restrict its scope. The amended bill was passed by the Senate in October 1970 and sent to the Chamber of Deputies for approval. Again the Vatican intervened. Pope Paul VI denounced the pending legislation vigorously. Nevertheless, on November 30 the Chamber passed the amended bill and sent it to President Saragat for his signature. On December 18, 1970, the Fortuna-Baslini bill became law. Divorce, under heavily restrictive conditions, had come to Italy, one hundred years after the Italian kingdom had ended the temporal power of the popes.

In this atmosphere of radical social change, political terrorism overtook the country. In the immediate aftermath of the second world war, the country had witnessed occasional violence. Later pan-German or pan-Austrian activists had committed isolated terrorist acts in the South Tyrol—bombings of utilities and power lines for the most part—to reinforce demands for separation from Italy. At their worst these had been random or spasmodic acts of violence. Following the disorders of the student movement in 1968 terrorism became a key political tactic of extremist groups holding a variety of political positions but a shared antagonism to the parliamentary republic. They would be given or would themselves assume labels such as right-wing Fascist or extremist Communist, but their contempt for order and the rules of the democratic game gave them much in common, even when attacking each other. Their kind of terrorism was different in nature and degree from what had been experienced before.

In a few months at the end of 1968 and in early 1969 a growing number of minor episodes threatened public order. The serious violence began in the spring. On April 25, 1969, the twenty-fourth anniversary of the liberation of northern Italy from Nazi-Fascist rule, two bombs exploded in Milan, wounding nineteen people. On August 9, 1969, explosives were set off on eight trains in various parts of Italy, mostly in the north. In autumn 1969 violence in the factories increased in connection with the negotiation of new trade union contracts. Clashes between students and police or between workers and police intensified, and in October and November of that year a student and a police agent lost their lives.

December 12, 1969 inaugurated a new era. On that day during normal business hours a highly destructive bomb was set off in the branch of the Bank of Agriculture on Piazza Fontana in Milan, killing 16 and injuring 90 people. The same day three bombs exploded in Rome, injuring 16 persons though no lives were lost. The bombing in Piazza Fontana set off a spiral of terrorist acts that had not ended ten years later. The investigation of the crime dragged on. An anarchist, Pietro Valpreda, was initially arrested and charged; the evidence against him was weak but he was held for years. The parties of the left accused the police and the government of using him as a scapegoat to protect the true miscreants, alleged to be extreme neo-Fascists who were acting on secret military or police intelligence instructions. The left charged that a "strategy of tension" was being orchestrated by unnamed powers located in high places. After Valpreda was released for lack of evidence the search continued. Finally two young former neo-Fascists, Franco Freda and Giovanni Ventura, were arrested for the crime. In February 1979, almost ten years later, they were found guilty and sentenced to life imprisonment.

NOTES

1. Gianni Statera, *Death of a Utopia: The Development and Decline of Student Movements in Europe* (New York: Oxford University Press, 1975).

2. Massimo Teodori, *The New Left: A Documentary History* (Indianapolis: Bobbs-Merrill, 1969).

6

TRADE UNION DEVELOPMENTS

The Italian trade union confederations had been weak and ineffective throughout the 1950s. Their weakness was the result of the divisions within the trade union movement that were based on political affiliations. Even more it was a consequence of chronic high unemployment. An additional source of debility was the concentration of bargaining power at the national level. Collective bargaining was conducted between the national headquarters and the highest-level organizations of employers such as Confindustria. Agreements at the firm or plant level were illegal, although, in fact, they did occur. During the 1950s average real wages had risen more slowly than average productivity, permitting the growth of profits, which, in turn, were invested in economic expansion.

During the years of the economic miracle, between 1959 and 1963, inemployment almost disappeared. Wage increases became more numerous and more generous. The bargaining power of the unions increased because of favorable economic conditions and because the trade unions concentrated more on the bread-and-butter questions of wages and working conditions and less on the rivalries engendered by their political party linkages. Rival unions collaborated informally. The 1962 round of negotiations for the renewal of the standard three-year contracts produced some good settlements and initiated changes in relationships and procedures. For the first time the contracts provided for plant-level bargaining on a restricted number of issues within well-defined rules. The big change came later, in 1968 and 1969, when the procedures were revised to provide for across-the-board collective bargaining with the firm.[1]

A consequence of the shift in locus of collective bargaining negotiations was the weakening of the power of the large employer associations, particularly the most important of them, Confindustria. The Confederation of Industries had already been hurt by the detachment of the publicly controlled corporations from the association in 1957, and their reorganization into the association called Intersind. In 1962 Intersind settled first with the unions on terms that Confindustria had rejected. Next the Fiat Corporation broke the united front of the private industrialists and reached its own agreement with the metal mechanics union. Finally, in February 1963, Confindustria settled with the unions on the basis of conditions already agreed to by Intersind and Fiat. For the first time the increases in salary were larger than the increase in productivity.[2] The 1968 changes were a logical outgrowth of the trends begun earlier.

Bargaining at the plant level benefited the workers in the more profitable firms and industries. It encouraged differentiation of rewards and increased the gaps among trade union members and between them and nonmembers. During the same period, however, through both labor contracts and legislation, certain previously accepted differentiations were eliminated. Separate salary scales based on sex were abolished. In 1969 salary scales based on geographical zones were outlawed. In 1973 separate scales based on age were eliminated; in the same year wage scales were equalized between white-collar and blue-collar workers.

The elimination of the differences based on geographical zones was done in the name of justice for the southern workers. In bringing their wages to the level of the rest of the country, however, the program for the development of the south was threatened. For many industries the only attraction the south had been able to offer was lower labor costs, and this advantage was now wiped out. To preserve the southern development program, the government passed new laws shifting the costs of financing certain welfare and fringe benefits from the firms' wage package to the national treasury. In other words, the general public, rather than the businesses, would bear the cost. By compensating the firms for the higher wages to be paid, the inducement to invest in the south would remain. At the same time it was expected that the increase in southern incomes would raise the demand for goods and services and further stimulate economic growth.

The gains the workers obtained over the decade were offset to an extent by short-run cyclical fluctuations and by long-run structural trends. The economic downturn in the years from 1963 through 1965 brought an end to the period of relatively full employment and concomitant increases in wages. The trade unions entered the 1965-66 round of contract negotiations in a much weaker position; the resulting agreements reflected this situation. The wage and salary increases gained were small, averaging about 5 percent, with specialized and skilled workers doing a little better. The unions achieved only limited success in preventing layoffs, whether on an individual or a collective basis, either through contract provisions or through legislation. By 1968 they did gain new laws setting unemployment compensation in industry at 80 percent of wages for three months, with retention of full family allowances. This legislation cushioned the material hardships if not the psychological blow of losing a position.

If the workers received little from the 1965-66 collective bargaining agreements, the union organizations achieved important gains. The most significant was the checkoff. Union dues would be deducted from the member's paycheck, thereby providing the unions with a steady and large source of income that they had never had before. Throughout the early postwar period the unions had been dependent on the voluntary payment of dues. In their competitive struggles for membership they did not expel delinquents. The resultant poverty of the organizations kept them dependent for financial support on the political parties with which they were associated. The non-Communist-dominated union confederations, CISL and UIL, were also receiving funds from the American and international trade union movements and also indirectly from the CIA. The achievement of a regular income through the checkoff established an important prerequisite for the subsequent efforts of the trade unions to cut their ties with the political parties and foreign sources of support.

In addition to the financial gains the unions acquired the right to have union newspapers posted on plant bulletin boards, the use of plant offices for union business, and similar benefits that collectively augmented the presence of the trade unions in the plants.

The emergence of national democratic programming found the unions ambivalent at best. CISL and UIL, identified with the political parties of the center-left coalition, were reserved in their expressions of opinion, but CGIL was openly hostile. The Socialist minority in CGIL, although linked to the second largest party of the coalition, was unable or unwilling to restrain the Communist majority from its critical attacks. All the unions could applaud the plan's priority on achieving full employment. They objected to, and CGIL openly opposed, the initial version of the plan that included provisions for an incomes policy. These provisions would have limited wage settlements to the average increase in labor productivity to keep prices and labor costs stable. The unions considered an incomes policy a euphemism for a wage freeze without any corresponding limitations imposed on employers. The Italian trade union movement never accepted an incomes policy in principle. By 1969 events made it irrelevant. Confindustria accepted the idea of programming reluctantly, but opposed the plan that emerged in 1966 for reasons opposite to those of the unions. It centered its attack on the priority given to full employment rather than to economic efficiency.

Democratic programming required the collaboration of the trade union movement as well as business. That was inherent in the nature of the plans and in the planning machinery, since representatives of the union confederations sat on the committees participating in the development of the plans. The cool reception the trade union organizations gave to programming indicated the varying degrees of their unwillingness to become integrated into the political and economic system.

CGIL was still the largest confederation throughout the 1960s, although its membership was declining. Meanwhile CISL succeeded in achieving a slow but steady growth during the decade. The membership of UIL remained stagnant. Despite differing philosophical and political origins and despite the competition for membership, the major confederations had found it beneficial to collaborate on concrete issues in their negotiations with employers and their associations. Unity of action on specific problems might be extended to broader approaches. The possibility of reunification of the divided union movement emerged. The larger cultural and political atmosphere encouraged such a hope. The influence of Pope John XXIII and Vatican Council II, particularly the Vatican's extension of friendship to nonbelievers and encouragement of dialogue with those of differing philosophical inspiration, provided a favorable context. The formation of the center-left coalition and the political collaboration between Catholics and Socialists was another positive factor.

The links between the confederations and the political parties remained a stumbling block. If reunification were to materialize, these links would have to be severed to guarantee that the reunified confederation could not be dominated and manipulated by a political party. A critical element of this linkage was the leading position held by trade union officials in party and governmental organizations. At the top of the union hierarchy were officers who were also members of parliament, of the central committees and national councils, and of the executive boards of the political parties. Further down the hierarchy union officials held office in the provincial party federations or in provincial and municipal governments. CISL supported Forze nuove, a well-identified faction within the DC. Furthermore, top officers such as Giulio Pastore and Carlo Donat Cattin were cabinet ministers in numerous DC and center-left governments.

It was CISL that initiated the moves to loosen the ties with the government and subsequently with the DC. At its 1965 convention the delegates resolved that CISL officers could not hold posts in the cabinet, whether as ministers or undersecretaries. Pastore, who was quite old, retired. Donat Cattin resigned his office in CISL, preferring to remain the leader of Forze nuove. In subsequent years the ban was extended so that by 1969 CISL officers were precluded from running for parliament or for provincial, municipal, and regional councils (in the five special regions). They were also forbidden to be officers in the apparatus of the political parties. Beyond these prohibitions the 1969 convention also ordered that CISL no longer urge its members to vote for DC.

An analogous process was at work in ACLI, the Christian Association of Italian Workers. This organization was not a trade union but an educational and social agency linked to the Catholic Action Society, which is under the guidance of the bishops. In the late 1960s ACLI, led by the dynamic Catholic activist Livio Labor, was moving to the left. In June 1969 a majority at its annual convention voted to cut ACLI's ties to the Catholic Action Society and to abolish the practice of having chaplains attached to the association's chapters. Ties to the DC would also be cut. ACLI members would no longer run for political office on DC election lists. The association announced that its members were free to vote for whichever party they wished. Resistance to these developments by more traditional elements induced Labor to resign from ACLI to form a new political movement of the extreme left, ACPOL, the Christian Association for Labor Political Action. He was to convert it later into a political party for the 1972 parliamentary elections.[3]

Parallel developments were taking place in UIL, historically tied to the Social Democrats and, to a lesser degree, the Republicans. The unification of the Socialists and Social Democrats into the PSU in 1966 had created a situation in which PSU trade unionists were now divided, some in CGIL and others in UIL. The unification agreement permitted Socialist trade unionists to choose their trade union confederation. By the time of the PSU split in July 1969 a left-wing group led by Giorgio Benevento had gained control of UIL. After the split most of the UIL leaders and members decided not to return to the PSDI but to join the PSI. In the same year UIL also forbade its officials to hold political party or governmental offices.

CGIL, predominately Communist with a PSI minority, was the slowest to make the move initiated by CISL. Ties to the political parties were historic and strong. For many Communist unionists the party, not the union, was the mother. Union office was part of a party career. In this period the PCI endorsed the principle of trade union unity and independence but found it hard to put the endorsement into practice. The developments in the other confederations forced the issue, however; and CGIL went part of the way traveled by the others. Overcoming the resistance of orthodox Communist labor leaders such as its president, Agostino Novella, CGIL voted at its 1969 convention to prohibit its top leaders from being members of parliament or holding party office at the national level. Luciano Lama and other top CGIL Communists resigned from the Chamber of Deputies and from the Executive Bureau of the PCI. Below the national level, however, joint officeholding was still permitted.[4]

These developments did not mean, of course, that either the voting habits of union members or their personal or political relations were drastically altered. Union leaders might no longer be subject to party discipline, inside or outside a legislature, but reciprocal influences continued. The degree of separation varied, but in all three confederations, in CGIL least of all, the union leaders established an autonomy from the parties that enabled them to propose policies and take actions during the 1970s that would have been most unlikely at an earlier time. The premises had been laid for unity of action and for prospective reunification, but obstacles remained.

Among these obstacles was the evolution of economic conditions in Italy in the late 1960s, particularly in the manufacturing industries. The economic revival that began at the end of 1965 led to increased industrial productivity but to little increase in industrial employment. The improved productivity was the result of a reorganization of work procedures and a speedup of industrial techniques. Industrial employment reached a peak in 1966 and from that time forward remained relatively stable. Industrial patterns were changing, however. The number of large firms (over 500 employees) remained stationary, while the number of medium-sized (100 to 500 employees) and small (10 to 100 employees) firms grew. The tiny artisan-level shops (fewer than 10 employees) were as numerous as ever. Consequently, a larger proportion of the labor force employed in manufacturing was working for the small and medium-sized firms and a smaller proportion in the large firms.

Meanwhile, big industry was experiencing a concentration of control. Government-controlled businesses were being brought under one or more of the principal super-holding agencies: IRI and ENI, plus the nationalized electric power trust, National Electric Power Agency (ENEL). In the private sector five or six major conglomerates emerged, of which Fiat was the largest. There were also large conglomerates, such as Montedison, in which ownership was almost equally divided between private stockholders and government super-holding agencies. Moreover, the large manufacturing plants were contracting out various parts of the production process more commonly than before. The strongholds of the union movement had always been in the large manufacturing plants, and contracting out, which the unions had little success in blocking, complicated their problems of organizing and controlling the work force.

The stagnation of the overall size of the work force employed in industry did not mean a low turnover rate. As many workers left manufacturing for service jobs, a new influx of rural immigrants to the industrial cities replaced them, exacerbating the life of urbanites and immigrants alike: creating more congestion, more housing problems, and more social, educational, and recreational problems. The rural immigrants were less skilled than their predecessors and less accustomed to the discipline of the factory system. By 1967 unskilled workers comprised 23.9 percent of all industrial workers, with 25.8 percent in the manufacturing plants. In the automobile industry they comprised 45.6 percent of the total, with 65 percent unskilled workers at the Fiat plants in Turin.[5]

The vexations of life and of work in the large industrial centers and the limited gains obtained by the unions in the 1965-66 round of collective bargaining negotiations provided the background for the growing unrest in the industrial plants. It was the infection of the violence of the student movement in 1968 and 1969, however, that precipitated the upheavals in the factories. The example of the substantial gains achieved by the French workers in May and June 1968 when they linked their strikes to the French student uprising provided an additional stimulus.

Extremist Italian students had shifted their focus of activities from the universities to the plants as part of their attack on all social and political structures. Most of the workers were indifferent to the ideas and goals of the student agitators but were susceptible to the atmosphere of revolt. The students preached strange mixtures of classical Marxism, Catholic romanticism inherited from the worker-priest movement, revolutionary syndicalism, and Marcusian new-left slogans. By late 1968 the first "unitary rank-and-file committees" were being formed in the plants by young workers and students to press the workers' demands; these committees not only existed apart from union control, but also in many respects they were anti-union.

With the 1969 negotiations for renewal of the labor contracts, the struggle came to a climax in the "hot autumn" of that year. The conflict was more persistent and more violent than at any time since the occupation of the factories in 1920. More hours of work were lost; more people were involved than at any previous period of contract renewals. In many cases the workers engaged in wildcat strikes or blocked a section of a plant or a whole plant, leaving their union leaders far behind. Strikes were prolonged beyond the length of time fixed by the unions; demands were raised beyond the original claims of the leadership. Extremist assemblies composed of worker and student members condemned bosses and unions alike, shouting slogans such as "more money, less work" or "a contract is a piece of paper."

In these circumstances the major labor confederations were forced to join their worker antagonists, adopt many of the demands of the rank-and-file committees, and participate in the upheavals in order to regain their positions. CGIL was the first to adjust; the others followed. In the process the confederations collaborated with one another in the elections of workers' delegates to factory councils and to unitary assemblies. This collaboration to regain control of the situation helped overcome traditional divisions among the confederations and further stimulated the movement toward trade union unity.

Employers were outraged and frightened, but found little support from the DC minority government. The one-party DC cabinet, now headed by Mariano Rumor, was too weak to control labor unrest and maintain order. The PCI and PSI naturally supported the unions, and the Rumor cabinet was concerned to obtain a settlement on almost any terms. Throughout the 1960s the minister of labor had played an increasingly important role in collective bargaining negotiations. During the hot autumn the minister of labor was Carlo Donat Cattin, formerly of CISL, who exerted the strongest pressures to overcome employer resistance. He directed his initial efforts to the firms in the public sector of the economy, grouped together in Intersind. They capitulated first, under political pressure, and this capitulation made it harder for Confindustria to hold out. Employers' worries about their ability to absorb the increased costs of production were assuaged by government promises to subsidize their losses. By the end of 1969 the hot autumn was over, but its effects would be felt in 1970 and the next decade.

Organized labor's gains were the highest ever achieved at any one time. In 1970, the first year under the new agreements, industrial wages rose 18.3 percent. In 1971 and 1972 they increased further, by 9.8 percent and 9.0 percent respectively. The indexing mechanism linking wage increases to the cost of living was improved. There was a general acceptance of the forty-hour work week, controls on overtime work, and a simplification of the different levels and distinctions among categories of workers. The overall result was to reduce the wage spread among specialized, skilled, semi-skilled, and unskilled workers, a result contrary to the 1966 settlements. The principal beneficiaries, however, were the full-time workers in the large plants. Gaps in wages and benefits actually widened between the lucky and unlucky ones: between those with jobs in the large firms and those in the small firms, between factory workers and cottage labor, between those holding secure jobs and those whose employment was precarious, between full-time and part-time workers.

In 1970 parliament passed a comprehensive body of labor legislation reflecting the atmosphere and the outcome of the hot autumn. It legislated many of the gains achieved in collective bargaining agreements and extended them to other categories of the labor force. It gave the workers almost complete protection from employer control: for example, the number of days of permissible sick leave was greatly expanded, while employers were prevented from checking on the validity of the absence. The law established the principle of just cause for individual or group firings or layoffs, laying the burden of proof on the employer. The results of the law and of the atmosphere were an increase in absenteeism, a reduction of discipline in the plants, and a general decline of productivity.[6]

The hot autumn brought victory to the major trade unions. Recovering from their initial loss of control over the workers they reasserted their presence and influence, both in the factories and in the larger society. Membership grew; for example, CGIL had 2.63 million members in 1969 and counted 3.44 million members by 1973.[7] The collaboration of the confederations during the crisis furthered the progress toward reunification. On May 1, 1970, the unions held one joint May Day celebration. In October of the same year they met to discuss formal reunification but discovered that this goal was still premature. The following year they met again, found that considerable differences still remained over the question of political affiliations, but agreed in principle to unite by 1973. In that year, however, the remaining divergences blocked the final step. Instead, they agreed to establish a federation of the confederations, which they named CGIL-CISL-UIL, a compromise that was to endure despite varying strains and disappointments.

Although unity eluded the three confederations, they collaborated on political action. Extending their scope from traditional subjects of union action the confederations agreed, beginning in 1970, to concentrate their efforts on modifying government social policies. They decided to bypass the political parties and parliament to achieve social reform. The primary fields of their activity were health, education, housing, social security, and transportation. Their primary weapon, the strike, was used generously in 1970. In October of that year the cabinet agreed to establish one national health service to replace a number of separate health programs, to build more public housing, to improve public transportation, to expand the school system, and to raise old-age pensions. All these reforms were justifiable; they were also expensive. Not surprisingly, their implementation was delayed and the scope of the promises reduced.

For the unions the emphasis on social reforms was, in a sense, a continuation on a national scale, in the larger society, of the struggle in the factories. The mass of unionized workers could be pleased with the immediate and concrete results of their action. For the small number of extremists, however, the hot autumn had been intended to launch an attack to overthrow the system. The unions' shift in emphasis to social reform appeared to the extremists to be a cooptation of the workers into the system. Workers' participation in the making of governmental social and economic policies results in their defending those policies. This reduces their fighting spirit and hostility to the political and economic order, when on the contrary, the workers should always be on the attack. Consequently the revolutionary minority opposed, but without success, the emergence of the trade union movement as an active autonomous protagonist in the political process. Since the unions and most of the workers could not support the revolutionaries, the extremist minority turned to disruptive and terrorist tactics, trying to achieve a state of permanent conflict, in the plants and in the broader society.

NOTES

1. Vittorio Foa, "Sindacati e classe operaia," in *L'Italia contemporanea 1945-1975*, ed. Valerio Castronovo (Turin: Einaudi, 1976), p. 267.

2. Gloria Pirzio Ammassari, *La politica della Confindustria* (Naples: Liguori, 1976), pp. 108-11.

3. Giuseppe Mammarella, *L'Italia dalla caduta del fascismo ad oggi* (Bologna: Il Mulino, 1978), p. 455.

4. Peter Weitz, "The CGIL and the PCI: From Subordination to Independent Political Force," in *Communism in Italy and France*, ed. Donald L. M. Blackmer and Sidney Tarrow (Princeton: Princeton University Press, 1975), pp. 541-71.

5. Foa, "Sindacati e classe operaia," p. 273.

6. Giorgio Galli, "La politica italiana," in AA. VV., *Dal '68 a oggi come siamo e come eravamo* (Bari: Laterza, 1979), p. 73.

7. Foa, "Sindacati e classe operaia," p. 261.

7

POLITICAL STRESSES

The minority Christian Democratic cabinet that had ineffectually faced the violence of the hot autumn of 1969 came into being after the Socialist split had caused the breakdown of the center-left coalition. Prime Minister Rumor failed to reconstitute the coalition because the aftermath of their rupture left the two Socialist parties intensely hostile to each other. The bombing in the Piazza Fontana, however, which appeared to threaten the survival of the political system, made it incumbent on the politicians to create a more broadly based cabinet. Negotiations were begun to that end.

The alternative was to dissolve parliament and call new elections. Liberals and Social Democrats favored this choice, expecting that a popular reaction to the disorders of the two previous years would work in their favor. For the same reason the Socialists and Communists were resolutely opposed. Because the Christian Democrats were weak and divided they had no desire to face an election in the spring of 1970, especially since provincial and local elections regularly scheduled for the summer could provide an indication of the humor of the electorate. In retrospect it is now clear that dissolving parliament in the 1969-70 winter would have exacerbated the tensions and atmosphere of crisis. In any case, the Christian Democratic refusal put an end to talk of parliamentary dissolution: attention shifted to the necessity of constructing another coalition government.

A return to the centrist coalitions of the 1950s, bringing the Liberal Party back into the government to replace the Socialists, was numerically possible. Although the Social Democrats were initially favorable, the idea encountered resistance from their former partners. Gradually but inexorably, a reconstitution of the four-party center-left government emerged as the only feasible solution. Between January and March attempts by Rumor, Moro, and Fanfani to form a cabinet failed. The critical issue was the relationship of the center-left to the Communists, in parliament and in the country. Social Democrats and many Christian Democrats insisted on isolating the Communists at all governmental levels. But in numerous local administrations the Socialists had been allied to the Communists rather than to center-left parties before and during the heyday of the center-left. In several localities Communists and Socialists in a popular front coalition provided the only numerical majority. If the two left parties did not form a government the local administrations would have had to be taken over by a prefectural commissioner until new elections were called. In addition the left factions within the Socialist Party were tepid at best to a reconstitution of the four-party coalition. For these reasons the PSI had no intention of making a radical change now. The impasse was resolved by the Christian Democratic secretary-general, Arnaldo Forlani, whose elastic and ambiguous formula emphasized the obligation of center-left consistency and gave the Socialists the freedom to make the choices they wished after the forthcoming local elections.

During the peak period of the center-left coalitions the historic strains over church-state issues, although somewhat moderated, persisted between Socialists and Christian Democrats. In the late 1960s special privileges of the Vatican came under increasing attack from the left. In 1967 the Socialists challenged the Vatican's nonpayment of income taxes on dividends from Italian investments. These dated from the Lateran Accords of 1929 under which the Italian state had made a large financial reimbursement to the Holy See in settlement of the Roman Question. The Vatican became the controlling stockholder in several large firms, such as the Società Generale Immobiliare, the largest real estate company in Italy. It was the most important minority stockholder in the IRI Banco di Roma. Although Italian law did not exempt the Church from paying income taxes on its earnings in Italy, successive DC treasury ministers used administrative fiat to waive the Holy See's financial obligation to the national state. In 1967 the Socialists forced the DC hand on this question. The Christian Democrats conceded. Informed that it would have to start paying taxes, the Vatican began to sell off its Italian stockholdings and to invest the proceeds outside the country.

The wrangling on this issue stimulated the secular forces to agitate for revision of the Concordat between Italy and the Holy See.

Because the Concordat is an international treaty, its revision requires the consent of both parties. At the end of the decade the government appointed a special committee of ecclesiastical experts to study the question. The Vatican did the same. In the meantime, the 1970 vote in the Chamber on the Fortuna-Baslini divorce bill and the Vatican's intervention to block the vote created a new obstacle to resolution of the government crisis. The most the DC, in a minority on this issue, could do was to delay Senate passage until the fall. Fanfani tried to form a government based on a commitment by the prospective lay partners to pass a bill implementing the process of a referendum, which would then be used to attempt an overturn of the anticipated divorce law. Fanfani also insisted that the secretaries-general of the four parties participate personally in the cabinet to form a directorate with him to guarantee the stability of his government and the loyal backing of the parties. Fearing the subordination of the secretaries to the prime minister, the other parties, and the DC as well, rejected his proposed innovation. Fanfani withdrew and Rumor again came to the fore, proposing Forlani's compromise and Fanfani's linkage of the divorce bill to the referendum act. On this basis Rumor was finally able to establish a new cabinet on March 27, 1970, consisting of 17 Christian Democrats, six Socialists, three Social Democrats, and one Republican. The cabinet received votes of confidence from the two houses of parliament on April 10 and April 17. The crisis had been one of the lengthiest and most difficult of the postwar period.[1]

The duration of the cabinet crisis in no degree matched the period of inaction on the referendum question. Article 75 of the 1948 constitution provided for the institution of a popular referendum to repeal laws, in whole or in part. For 22 years successive Italian governments had blocked the required implementing legislation, defeating all opposition attempts to institute a referendum. As long as the DC dominated parliament, it was determined to keep control over the legislative process. Now, while the Christian Democrats were losing control and passage of a divorce bill appeared inevitable, a series of opinion polls indicated that a popular majority in the country, especially strong among women, opposed divorce. The DC parliamentarians rapidly shifted their tactics, and in the spring of 1970 legislation to implement a referendum was passed.

Further blows to Catholic doctrine were in store for the DC and the Holy See to be delivered by the Constitutional Court. In December 1970 the Court overthrew the historic law on adultery on the grounds that it discriminated against women, violating their constitutional right to equal treatment. Three months later, on grounds of freedom of speech and freedom of the press, the Court overturned a 1926 Fascist law that prohibited the publication and dissemination of information on birth control. Both decisions reflected the growing secularization of Italian public life.

In the spring of 1970 parliament passed two other important laws, the labor relations act described earlier and the final bill instituting governments for the 15 regular regions. Here again it took 22 years to implement a provision of the constitution completely (Articles 115 to 133). The five special regional governments had been created in the early postwar period because of the presence of either linguistic minorities, as in the Vald'Aosta, Trentino-Alto Adige, and Friuli-Venezia Guilia, or separatist movements, as in Sicily and Sardinia. Then the process of establishing regional governments had ground to a halt, in spite of a Christian Democratic tradition favoring decentralization and regionalism that went back to the earlier years of the twentieth century. The Communist and Socialist movements had no such tradition; on the contrary they reflected the Jacobin preference for the unitary centralized state. The Christian Democrats, in continuous control of the national government, had no interest in creating institutions that might weaken this control, and therefore ignored the constitution and their own tradition. The Marxist parties became entrenched in the Red Belt—the regions of Emilia-Romagna, Tuscany, and Umbria—while their prospects for victory at the national level dwindled. So they reversed their positions and became champions of regionalism, hoping for gains below the national level.

When center-left coalition governments emerged in the 1960s the Socialists included implementation of the constitutional provisions for the regions among their conditions for participation. It was not a critical condition, however, and the DC was successful in postponing action. In the late 1960s a number of Christian Democrats rediscovered their regionalist heritage and in 1968 parliament passed a law providing for the establishment of governments in the 15 normal regions. Since the law made no provisions for election procedures or for financing these governments, it was useless. Violence in the final years of the decade, particularly in the hot autumn of 1969, was probably the determining factor in the Christian Democratic decision to pass the financing act and the electoral law in the spring of 1970. The first election to establish regional councils was set for June 7 of that year. The elected councils then had to draft regional constitutions and get them approved by the national parliament. At the same time they had to build a bureaucracy that, in large part, was composed of employees transferred from the national government.

The time consumed in these necessary first steps meant that the governments did not begin to operate until the spring of 1972.

The regional governments were organized on a parliamentary system. The regional council, a unicameral legislature elected by proportional representation with the preference vote, would create a cabinet, the *giunta*, led by the president of the region. The president, the equivalent of a prime minister at the national level, and his *giunta* would need a vote of confidence from the regional council. The term of office of the council was five years.

The parties devoted the late spring of 1970 to the election campaign. In addition to the 15 new regional councils, large numbers of provincial and communal governments were up for their regular elections. June 7, therefore, would be the first important indication of how the Italian public felt about the upheavals of the preceding two years. The novelty and significance of the new level of government were lost in an atmosphere of debate over national political issues, including the capacity of the government to maintain law and order.

This last theme was emphasized particularly by the neo-Fascists. After the death in 1969 of its leader, Arturo Michelini, who represented the moderate wing, the MSI had become more extremist. Succeeding him as secretary-general was Giorgio Almirante, the spokesman of the revolutionary faction, who favored policies analogous to the squadrist activities of Fascism in 1921-22, before the march on Rome. Almirante had been an official in the Republic of Salò, Mussolini's government of the Fascist Social Republic set up behind the Nazi lines in northern Italy during 1943-44. His emphasis was on national socialism. Some of the student groups active in 1968 and 1969 were offshoots of his wing of the party. At the same time that neo-Fascist elements were contributing to the terrorism, the MSI was denouncing the government for its failure to maintain law and order. It expected to benefit electorally from the average citizen's fears and frustrations.

Missini expectations were fulfilled in part. In the June 7 election it received 5.2 percent of the vote, in comparison to the 4.3 percent it received in the 1968 parliamentary election in the 15 regions, a noticeable but not exceptional gain. The PCI vote remained static compared to 1968, although the party usually did better in administrative than in parliamentary elections. The DC vote declined a little; it usually did poorer in administrative elections. The conspicuous gainers were the Social Democrats and the Socialists, running separately after their split of the previous year. They regained almost all the votes they had had in 1964, before they merged in 1966. This election confirmed their split, if only in purely vote-getting terms. But the sources of their gains were from different parts of the electorate. The PSDI benefited from the law-and-order reaction, while the PSI, in moving to the left after 1969, recaptured votes from PSIUP, its 1964 leftist offshoot. The Italian Socialist Party of Proletarian Unity was declining; its reason for existence became obsolete once the PSI moved again toward collaboration with the PCI.

The 1970 elections demonstrated once more the basic stability of the Italian electorate. For a party to gain or lose 1 percent of the total vote is considered noteworthy. For a small party like the MSI, with only slightly more than 4 percent of the vote, the gain of almost one percentage point meant an increase of 21 percent over its previous vote, enough to stimulate its militants to continued activity. Another, and important, consequence of the election was the significant shift in the composition of many local governments. In the three Red Belt regions the Socialists joined with the Communists to form popular front regional governments, while in most of the other regions they allied with the DC and smaller parties to form center-left coalitions. In several provinces and communes, however, the Socialists switched from center-left to popular front coalitions, thereby bringing the Communists into control of a number of local governments for the first time since the 1950s. The complexion of local government in Italy changed noticeably because of this shift in local alliances.[2]

The regional capitals were established in the principal cities of the regions, Milan in Lombardy, Rome in Lazio, Naples in Campania, for example. In two regions, however, rivalries between cities for location of the capital provoked riots. At stake were not only local patriotism but also jobs, contracts, real estate investments, and commercial growth, all associated with the establishment of government agencies and offices. In the Abruzzi the competitors were the cities of L'Aquila and Pescara. Rioting broke out in L'Aquila when it appeared that Pescara might be selected. Several party headquarters were assaulted and burned. Conceding to the violence, the government chose L'Aquila.

Far more serious was the situation in Calabria. There, at the toe of Italy's boot, three cities vied for the honor: Cosenza, Catanzaro, and Reggio Calabria. No one of them clearly dominated in size or historical tradition. Catanzaro, most centrally located, was initially designated as the capital. Protests from the other two cities forced the government not only to reconsider its choice but to enter into political negotiations to find a satisfactory compromise. Cosenza was compensated by the national government's promise to establish the new University of Calabria there.

In Reggio the situation was much worse. Rioting began in July 1970 and continued sporadically until February 1971. Barricades were set up in the streets. The neo-Fascists seized every opportunity to exploit the tensions and the hopes of the unemployed for jobs to fan the flames of discontent. Carabinieri battalions were brought to the city to restore order. After they were withdrawn rioting erupted again. Finally, the politicians found solutions that had no intrinsic justification other than to give something to each. The executive branch of the regional government—the *giunta* and the administrative agencies—was located at Catanzaro, but the regional council was established at Reggio Calabria. Moreover, IRI was to construct a major steel mill on the outskirts of Reggio, providing thousands of jobs in the area. Whether Italy needed another large steel mill, whether Reggio was the suitable location for it, were irrelevant questions; the politicians wanted only to get rid of a hot potato.

Subsequently, the government bought up large stretches of fertile farm land outside Reggio Calabria. Installation of the mill's infrastructure was begun. Then in the middle of the 1970s the worldwide steel depression began. Italy's existing mills were operating at only 60 percent of capacity. Work on the site was halted, but the government refused to admit that the mill would have to be abandoned. Only in 1979 in a manner as inconspicuous as possible did the government announce the cancellation of the steel mill in favor of other unspecified industries to be established at the Reggio site. Billions of lire had been wasted, and thousands of acres of fertile farm land destroyed.

The government that had administered the June 7, 1970 election survived it by only a month. On July 6 Prime Minister Rumor suddenly resigned, one day before a general strike scheduled by the unions to back up their demands for social reform. Rumor's cabinet, lasting a little over three months, had one of the shortest lives in postwar Italian history. In addition to the problems created by the continuing ferment among the workers, Rumor faced dissension within his own party; within his faction, the Dorotei; and between the Social Democrats and Socialists in his cabinet. Under the stimulus of the upheavals of 1969, the Social Democrats had shifted to a more conservative stance, to which they attributed their electoral gains. Meanwhile, the Socialists had shifted to the left, increasing their participation in local popular front coalitions. Their new secretary-general, Giacomo Mancini, was also trying to exploit student and worker militancy to his party's benefit; he interpreted his party's electoral gains as approval of his strategy. The Social Democrats accused the Socialists of violating the agreement of the early spring that had made the most recent center-left coalition possible. It is not surprising that Rumor felt he had had enough.

President Saragat first asked Giulio Andreotti, a competitor of Rumor within the Dorotei faction, to form a new center-left cabinet. The Socialists opposed him because they considered him too conservative. The Social Democrats feared him because they believed he had no ideological scruples and could easily make a public or covert deal with the PCI in spite of his conservatism. Andreotti withdrew his candidacy to be succeeded by Emilio Colombo, another Dorotei leader. Concern over economic conditions induced the parties to put aside their hostilities. Colombo quickly put together another center-left government that, by early August, easily obtained the confidence of both houses of parliament. Colombo had had many years of experience as treasury minister but this was his first investiture as prime minister.

The Colombo cabinet had to face changes in the psychological atmosphere. Although it was still possible to launch a demonstration against the U.S. war in Vietnam, the wave of extremism was petering out. Nevertheless tensions were rising throughout the country. Rioting in L'Aquila and Reggio Calabria revived historic southern feelings of resentment against the national government. In the north common criminality and violence increased. Vatican intervention in the parliamentary conflict over the divorce law strained relations between the DC and its lay partners.

The limited cohesion of the coalition parties was eroded throughout the last half of 1970 and all of 1971. The economic decline affected the political atmosphere. Christian Democratic factions were already beginning to maneuver in anticipation of the election of a new president of the republic, to be held at the end of 1971. In these circumstances the operations of the Colombo cabinet were reduced to little more than routine administration. In February 1971 the Republicans withdrew from the government, charging it with inaction and failure to control public expenditures. The Social Democrats and Socialists continued their squabbling, as the latter party edged closer to the Communists. The PCI was encouraging this evolution by avoiding intransigent attacks on the majority, in some cases actually helping the government (including the DC) by prudent abstentions.

Behind the PCI's soft approach was its increasing apprehension of widespread political unrest, which especially in the south benefited the neo-Fascists. For off-year local elections held in June 1971 in several cities and provinces scattered throughout Italy, the Missini conducted a vigorous and expensive campaign that paid off in a doubling and in some cases a tripling of its vote. It became the second largest party in the city of Catania (Sicily). MSI gains were most conspicuous in the south, where the DC and Liberals suffered significant losses to them. Christian Democracy, shaken by its defeat, made every effort to regain its influence and recover from the setback by shifting to a conservative stance. The shift was particularly important because of the forthcoming presidential election.

The seven-year term of office of President Saragat expired in December 1971. The president is elected by both houses of parliament in joint session, with added delegates from the regions. The Social Democratic president was old and sick but a candidate for reelection nonetheless. The DC, however, was determined to gain the office, but its lay partners opposed the leading party's ambition to control both the government and the presidency. The politicians spent the last half of 1971 completely on election maneuvering.

The presidential election was more than routine because the violence of recent years and the instability of cabinets had raised the question of institutional reform from the level of academic to political interest. Although parliamentary democracy had performed badly in Italy, in neighboring France a strong presidential republic appeared to manage problems efficiently. Connected with the election of the president, therefore, was the issue of the role the president should play and the powers a president should exercise.

Political forces fearful of the emergence of "a man on horseback" focused their concern on personal attributes; it was important that the winning candidate not be an ambitious person tempted to create a new and different political order. The 1948 constitution was a kind of social contract among Catholic, Marxist, and lay-liberal forces. Since DC domination of the political system was becoming shaky, the Marxist forces not surprisingly looked upon the establishment of a powerful president as a means to consolidate Christian Democratic control at their expense, perhaps a threat to their very survival. Many DC politicians also were suspicious of a presidential republic. They had operated the parliamentary system to their advantage for several decades; they knew all the techniques of maneuver and compromise; they had doubts about the utility of pushing the left into a position of intransigence. Although the parliamentary system was serving the country badly, the alternative could be worse.

Restructuring parliament drew some attention. Some commentators considered the Senate an unnecessary duplication of the Chamber of Deputies and advocated its abolition. It was difficult to imagine, however, that the Senate would vote itself out of existence. Others suggested that the Senate be elected on a corporatist rather than territorial basis to represent the various organized economic interests of the nation. Since most parliamentarians were old enough to remember Mussolini's corporate state, this suggestion received short shrift.

As the debate proceeded it became clear that neither a presidential republic nor parliamentary reform had significant political support. Italy needed a more effective executive but strengthening the authority of the prime minister and his cabinet depended on political forces and the personal qualities of leaders, not on institutional engineering.

Parliament assembled to elect a president on December 9, 1971. Saragat had the support of the Social Democrats, Republicans, and Liberals. Fanfani, presiding officer of the Senate, was the official DC candidate. Unofficially, Moro was available in case Fanfani faltered. The Socialists put forward their former secretary-general, De Martino, who had PCI support also since he would not necessarily reject a government supported by the Communists.

A two-thirds majority is required for election on the first three ballots; after that a simple majority is sufficient. Although the balloting is secret, it became apparent quickly that Fanfani was being deserted by some of his own Christian Democrats. Vote followed vote; days passed without a result. Moro, regarded with sympathy by the Marxist parties, had at least half of his own party against him. To break the stalemate, after the inconclusive twentieth ballot on December 21 the Christian Democrats put forward a compromise candidate, Giovanni Leone. The small parties that had endorsed Saragat promised to support Leone, but this was still not enough for victory. The Socialists substituted 80-year-old Nenni for De Martino. On the twenty-third ballot, held on December 24, Leone was elected. He took the oath of office on December 29. Almirante later claimed that MSI votes gave Leone the margin of victory.

Leone had been the speaker of the Chamber of Deputies and an interim prime minister. He had led caretaker minority DC cabinets after various breakdowns of center-left coalitions. He was not considered an important politician, nor was he a leader of a key faction of the DC. He was deemed safe; no one could imagine him, as they could Fanfani, trying to overturn the parliamentary system to establish a presidential regime.

The protracted election had left its mark on the country. As the Italian population watched one ballot follow another on television, the election process, the representative assemblies, and the parliamentary system fell into further disrepute. The situation was farcical, if not tragic. The two most important parties of the coalition, the DC and PSI, had opposed each other from beginning to end. Could the center-left coalition last much longer?

But when parliament reassembled on January 18, 1972, it was not Christian Democratic-Socialist conflict that brought the government down. The Republican Party had withdrawn from the cabinet the previous spring but had continued to support the center-left coalition as part of the majority in parliament. The PRI now removed its support, proclaiming that a new government was needed to take effective action on the nation's economic and social ills. The Republicans were especially worried about the rapid growth of public expenditures and the increasing deficit in the national budget. Prime Minister Colombo immediately presented his cabinet's resignation to President Leone.

Colombo then made some hesitant and feeble efforts to restore a four-party coalition, but differences between proponents of rigorous and of expansive economic policies led to failure. Leone then called on Andreotti. After going through similar motions Andreotti, with the president's approval, formed a one-party minority Christian Democratic cabinet that received the necessary endorsement of the former allies in parliament, and on February 18 was sworn into office. Ten days later Leone dissolved parliament, scheduling elections for May 7, 1972. For the first time in the history of the Italian republic parliament had been terminated before the completion of its five-year term.

Parliamentary support for Andreotti's caretaker government had been granted in anticipation of dissolution. For months sentiment had been growing among the parties for a new election. The main reason was the ubiquitous divorce issue. That question had returned to haunt the political compromise when militant Catholic groups gathered more than enough signatures to petition for a popular vote to repeal the divorce law. The referendum was scheduled for the spring of 1972. A feature of the referendum law provided for suspension of the popular vote if parliament was dissolved. Public opinion polls gave no clear indication of the outcome of the referendum. In the meantime the campaign would split the country apart. The DC would be in conflict with its smaller lay partners. Because the only other party in the country against the divorce law was the MSI, the DC would be uncomfortably coupled in the public mind with the neo-Fascists. For some time the PCI had been making approaches to the Christian Democrats, offering compromise amendments to the divorce law that the Catholic forces found unacceptable. The tensions generated by a nationwide referendum campaign would not only nullify the Communist approaches but also undermine the solidity of Communist supporters. The PCI drew votes from a large contingent of sympathizers whose attitudes on private-life and family questions were quite traditional.

The Socialists had done well in the regional and administrative elections of the two previous years and would hope for greater parliamentary representation. For a combination of reasons, therefore, the early dissolution of parliament seemed to the major parties to be a lesser evil than a referendum.

For more than two months the political life of the country was bound up in the parliamentary election campaign. The tiny Monarchist Party merged with the Neo-Fascists to form the Italian Social Movement-National Right (MSI-DN). The Manifesto faction, expelled from the PCI in 1969, launched its own slate, as did the dissident ACLI group led by Livio Labor. Other small extremist parties ran, for example, a group calling itself the Marxist-Leninist Communist Party.

The DC election strategy, bearing down heavily on the theme of law and order, stressed the centrality of the party to the political life of the country. In pinpointing its centrist position the DC was tacitly drawing back from the center-left policy it had pursued over the previous decade. The Communists fought their campaign on two fronts, trying to reach secular moderate and leftist Catholics with the theme of law and order and at the same time reemphasizing the revolutionary heritage to counter the attacks of the extraparliamentary left. The PSI accentuated reform, the importance of leftist unity, and the gains of the unions in recent years.

The neo-Fascists also played a double game. Under Almirante's leadership they emphasized respectability and law and order, playing down the violence of the nationalistic terrorist groups they had indirectly encouraged. On the MSI-DN electoral slate could be found high-level military officers and traditional bureaucrats together with squadrist and neo-Nazi elements.

The results of the May 7 election thwarted the hopes of the extremists, especially those of the left. None of the extraparliamentary groups succeeded in electing a single deputy or senator. The DC and PCI made slight gains compared to their 1968 parliamentary vote. The Social Democrats held their own. The limited Republican gains came principally at the expense of the Liberals. The PSI maintained the position it had won in the regional elections of 1970.

The MSI-DN made clear-cut but not extraordinary advances. The newly created party obtained 8.7 percent of the vote, far from the high point, 12.7 percent, that the Monarchists and neo-Fascists had reached separately in 1953. Nevertheless, the election doubled their representation in parliament over 1968. The third-largest party in Rome, the MSI-DN was also strong in some southern centers like Reggio Calabria and Catania.

The 1972 election gave a death blow to PSIUP. Having separated from the PSI in 1964 after the latter party joined the center-left, in the early 1970s, PSIUP found its supporters turning to the PSI or PCI. It received 1.9 percent of the votes on May 7 but they were so dispersed that not a single one of its 23 deputies was reelected. It elected 11 senators only because they ran on a joint ticket with the Communists. In a party congress held in July 1972 the PSIUP voted to dissolve. Almost two-thirds of the delegates joined the Communists, fewer than one-third returned to the PSI. A tiny minority, preferring to continue a separate existence, formed a new party, the Democratic Party of Proletarian Unity (PDUP). In the same period the dissident ACLI movement led by Livio Labor dissolved. Labor himself joined the Socialist Party.[3]

The years between 1968 and 1972 had witnessed the most destablizing events in postwar Italian history. Yet this ferment appeared to have little effect on the voting behavior of the electorate. The extremist movements demonstrated that they were more noisy than large. Of course, the constancy of the election returns, particularly for the large parties, hid internal changes that cancelled each other out. For example, the Communist gains from former PSIUP voters at the national level helped to compensate the PCI for losses to the neo-Fascists in the south. The DC had reasserted its critical role in the center of the political spectrum, showing once again its ability to mobilize voters' preferences for stability. Its task now was to organize a government capable of dealing with the changes occurring on the national and international economic scenes.

NOTES

1. Giuseppe Mammarella, *L'Italia dalla caduta del fascismo ad oggi* (Bologna: Il Mulino, 1978), pp. 465-68.

2. See the illustrated figure in Norman Kogan, "The Italian Communist Party: The Modern Prince at the Crossroads," in *Eurocommunism and Détente*, ed. Rudolf L. Tökés (New York: New York University Press, 1978), p. 88.

3. Norman Kogan, "Italy," in *World Topics Year Book 1973*, ed. Marilyn Robb Trier (Lake Bluff, Ill.: Tangley Oaks Educational Center, 1973), pp. 279-82.

8

ECONOMIC CRISES IN THE 1970s

A marked deterioration in the economic situation beginning in 1970 heightened political and social tensions in Italy. The downturn started sooner and the consequences were worse than in almost all of the other industrialized countries. For most of the next ten years the economy on the whole suffered high rates of inflation, major balance of payments difficulties, consequent severe devaluation of the lira, and low rates of real economic growth. In 1975, for the first time since World War II, the country underwent a recession rather than just a decline in its growth rate. The economic history of the decade was one of stop and go. Table 8.1 indicating the annual percentage changes in real gross national product, illustrates the pattern. With the exception of the slowdown in 1964-65, the real increases in the 1960s had been more than 5 percent a year. However, in the 1970s only three years, 1973, 1976, and 1979, saw a real GNP growth of more than 5 percent over the previous year.

World market prices of raw materials and foodstuffs, on which Italy was heavily dependent, had begun climbing in the years 1968-69. The consequences of the hot autumn began to be felt in 1970 as production costs rose faster than productivity. Self-financing of new investments had begun to drop in the late 1960s but the rate of decline accelerated in the early 1970s. Although the economy started to slow down in the summer of 1970, prices continued to rise. Table 8.2 shows the annual increases in consumer prices over the decade.

Faced with growing inflationary pressures the cabinet issued an executive decree in early September 1970 imposing new taxes, especially on consumption items. In addition, the decree changed various appropriations. When parliament returned from its summer

TABLE 8.1: Annual Changes in Real GNP in Italy, 1960-79

Year	Percentage Change Over Previous Year	Year	Percentage Change Over Previous Year
1960	—	1970	+5.0
1961	+8.2	1971	+1.6
1962	+6.2	1972	+3.1
1963	+5.6	1973	+6.9
1964	+2.6	1974	+3.7
1965	+3.2	1975	-3.9
1966	+5.8	1976	+5.5
1967	+7.0	1977	+2.1
1968	+6.3	1978	+3.0
1969	+5.7	1979	+5.6

Sources: Commercial Office of the Italian Embassy, Washington, D.C., *Italy, An Economic Profile, 1978*, p. 1; *Italy, An Economic Profile, 1979*, p. 1.

vacation it broke into an uproar over this usurpation of legislative powers. Under the Italian constitution the government may issue decrees in cases of an extreme emergency. Parliament then has 60 days to ratify or reject. Considering the cabinet's decree an abuse of its constitutional powers, parliament rejected the decree. The government then introduced a new decree with slightly changed language, thereby giving the taxes another 60 days of life. The opposition joined the allies of the DC to propose a deal: Parliament would ratify the decree if the Christian Democrats would let the divorce bill come to a vote. On November 28 the decree was ratified and on November 30 the Chamber of Deputies passed the divorce bill.

Confronted with continuing price rises the government imposed price controls on selected food items and certain basic supplies on September 22, 1971. Since no wage freeze was imposed, pressure on prices continued.

In August 1970 the United States had cut the dollar loose from gold and abandoned the dollar exchange standard. A year later, on August 15, 1971, the U.S. government devalued the dollar by 10 percent and, in addition, imposed a 10 percent surtax on imports. All exporters to the United States, including Italy, suffered from this increase in protectionism. Moreover, Italy was already under pressure to restrict its sales of shoes, textiles, and clothing in the American market. The United States had threatened to impose import quotas on these items if the Italians did not exercise self-restraint. In July 1971 Italy had reluctantly agreed to set its own limit on footwear sold to the United States. The drop in the value of the dollar

TABLE 8.2: Percentage Change in Consumer Prices for All Goods and Services in Italy, 1970-79

Year	1970	1971	1972	1973	1974	1975	1976	1977	1978	1979
Percentage Change	+5.0	+4.8	+5.7	+10.8	+19.1	+17.0	+16.8	+17.0	+12.1	+19.0

Sources: Commercial Office of the Italian Embassy, Washington, D.C., *Italy, An Economic Profile, 1975,* p. 3; and *Italy, An Economic Profile, 1978,* p. 2; *Italy, An Economic Profile, 1979,* p. 1.

the next month was a financial blow to the Italian treasury, which held a large amount of dollar reserves. Not surprisingly, in September the Italian government called for a new international currency exchange standard to replace the dollar reserve standard, a monetary system that would not be dominated by the currency of any one country. In subsequent years the International Monetary Fund did establish a system of special drawing rights (SDR), but neither the new system nor any other system has replaced the dollar as the principal reserve currency.

In the previous decade Italy had accumulated one of the largest reserves of gold and foreign exchange in the world. Still running a surplus in its current account in 1970 and 1971, the Italian government did not start to worry about its balance of payments soon enough. From 1972 to 1974 the country depleted its reserves severely. Table 8.3 summarizes Italy's annual payments balance for most of the 1970s. The deficits of 1972 and 1973 are the result of food and commodity price explosions. Since Italy imports 94 percent of its oil, mainly from the Middle East and North Africa, the massive deficit of 1974 is the consequence of the fourfold increase in the price of petroleum imposed by the Organization of Petroleum Exporting Countries (OPEC). The terms of trade had turned against Italy as the prices of its imports rose faster than the prices of its exports.

Italy's export problems resulted not only from occasional and sporadic protectionist impositions by other countries. New competitors emerged on the international market to challenge leading Italian export industries such as automobiles, shoes, and clothing. The last two industries met the challenge by concentrating on high quality and high style. The automobile industry was protected inside the Common Market but had trade difficulties elsewhere. Fiat rapidly diversified into nonautomotive products, but state-owned Alfa-Romeo was losing money heavily, particularly after 1972 when its Neapolitan plant, Alfa-Sud, came into production.

The 1972 trade union contract negotiations did not give rise to another hot autumn. In manufacturing, union gains above automatically indexed increases were modest. Without calling a major strike the metal mechanics union achieved the key settlement in October. The economic downturn and growing unemployment explain the restraint shown by the manufacturing unions. The situation was different in the services sector, where wages were inelastic. Throughout the fall and into 1973 price increases heightened discontent. In 1973 Italy's double-digit inflation was the highest in Western Europe. Wildcat strikes plagued the hotel and restaurant businesses and the public services: railways, municipal transportation, garbage

TABLE 8.3: Italy's Balance of Payments on the International Market, 1970-79

Year	1970	1971	1972	1973	1974	1975	1976	1977	1978	1979
Overall balance[a]	+356	+783	-1,281	-356	-5,518	-2,055	-1,235	+1,960	+8,244	+2,195

[a]in millions of dollars.
Sources: Commercial Office of the Italian Embassy, Washington, D.C., *Italy, An Economic Profile, 1975*, p. 5; *Italy, An Economic Profile, 1978*, p. 5; *Italy, An Economic Profile, 1979*, p. 5.

collection, mail deliveries, and electric power utilities. To add to the public unease, student demonstrators, Fascist and anti-Fascist, clashed in the city squares.

To offset the downturn the government had begun to pump money into the economy. By the end of 1972 and beginning of 1973 business was reviving, at the expense, however, of a large increase in private and public indebtedness. Profits had been declining for several years. By 1972 most big firms were losing money, or at best breaking even. Self-financed investments dwindled. In the private sector the alternative was to borrow from the banks. By 1973 the indebtedness of private sector firms had increased to 70 percent of total financing. Public firms used the endowment funds granted by the state to meet current expenses. These funds were supplements to all sorts of indirect subsidies already granted to firms in both sectors.

A substantial rise in government expenditures without a corresponding increase in tax revenues swelled the national debt. Subsidies to business were only one source of the increasing deficits. Until 1971 the public administration had operated at a surplus. Not only the national administration was spending more, so also were the local governments and the social security institutions. The governments were expanding services and were also hiring more employees to offset unemployment. By 1973 the proportion of government employees at all levels, from national to local, was one of the highest in Western Europe. Almost 30 percent of Italian workers were on a government payroll, as compared to 19 percent in West Germany, 14 percent in Belgium, and 13 percent in France. The deficits of the social security institutions from 1972 on were even higher than those of the local governments. These deficits reflected greatly improved health and pension benefits gained by the unions and subsequently extended to others by business and by the government. The national treasury had to cover the losses at all levels of public administration; the treasury cash deficit rose from 4.5 percent of gross domestic product in 1970 to 14.5 percent in 1975.[1]

In the main, the Bank of Italy financed the treasury deficits. The Bank had no choice but to expand the money supply, even though in doing so it lost control of the money supply. The resulting high rate of inflation was the subject of a major debate among economists. Although almost all of them agreed that the external forces, the increase of prices on world markets, was only a secondary cause, they disagreed over the major domestic sources of price increases. One school blamed the huge increase in labor costs of production after the 1969 union settlements, requiring governmental validation and large amounts of public funds to help businesses cover the costs of the higher wages and fringe benefits. The unions, in other words, imposed a burden on the country inconsistent with achieving price stability, full employment, and balance in the external accounts. The other school argued that excessive monetary expansion was the major cause of inflation and stagnation. It appears that in the early period, 1970-72, monetary expansion was overdone; it more than validated the increased labor costs in the effort to stimulate the economy. From 1973 on, however, both labor costs and money supply were pushing each other upward.[2].

The 1973 economic revival strained Italy's currency. The lira was already shaky in January. The Andreotti government, afraid to devalue openly, instituted a system of two rates, commercial and financial. Ordinary business transactions and tourist exchanges applied a rate of 580 lire to the dollar, at the same time that banks and other financial institutions could get 605 lire to the dollar. In February the U.S. dollar declined another 10 percent. Common Market treasury ministers met hurriedly. The majority decided to institute a common float against the dollar, called the snake and linked, essentially, to the strong German mark. Italy, Great Britain, and Ireland refused to join the snake. In the opinion of the Italian treasury minister, Giovanni Malagodi (Liberal Party) the lira was too weak to be revalued upward, which would be the result of participating in the common float. Consequently the lira fell independently almost as far as the dollar, 7 to 8 percent. Exports became more competitive but imports became more expensive, boosting prices in Italy. In June both the United States and the European Economic Community made loans to Italy to bolster the lira. Throughout the year, however, the lira's value fluctuated with the dollar.

By the summer of 1973 the economy was booming once more and so were prices. In July there were bread riots in Naples. The government reimposed selective price and rent freezes and began a credit squeeze. There were emergency importations of wheat, the appearance of black markets, and sporadic gasoline and fuel oil shortages.

Then in October came the Yom Kippur War between Israel and its Arab neighbors and the aftermath, the OPEC oil embargo. The government instituted a ban on driving in private cars on Sundays and holidays and other measures to reduce oil and gas consumption. Communists, Christian Democrats, and others clamored for a reconsideration of Italy's evenhanded foreign policy. The head of ENI, the National Hydrocarbons Agency, testified before the Foreign Affairs

Committee of the Chamber of Deputies that it was time for Italy to take a pro-Arab position. In the spring of 1974 ENI began making arrangements with Arab oil producers separate from oil-consuming nations' efforts at common action. One week after ENI completed an agreement with Libya, the Italian government called on Israel to return to the 1967 frontiers.

On December 25 the Arab oil producers ended the embargo for their customer nations except the United States and the Netherlands. The full impact of the fourfold increase in petroleum prices was felt in 1974. In Italy the automobile industry was hit hardest. Fiat had started losing money in 1973 for the first time in the postwar period, but 1974 losses were far worse. For much of the year Fiat operated on a three-day work week. The workers received supplements to their reduced wages from the unemployment compensation system so that they actually received between 80 and 90 percent of their full-time wages. The impact of the oil price rise was felt not only in the automotive industry but also in the manufacturing of plastics, fertilizers, and other petroleum by-products. At the end of 1973 British Petroleum sold its Italian subsidiary to the Monti Oil Company, a private firm. Early in 1974 ENI bought out most of the Italian operations of Royal Dutch Shell. Over the course of the year 70 percent of Italy's foreign payments went for oil.

When the lira began to float downward in early 1973, intervention by the Bank of Italy to support it had kept the decline moderate. During the first five months of 1974, the Bank lost foreign exchange at the rate of $1 billion a month. Italian commercial bank borrowing in the Eurocurrency market had reached $7 billion. At this point the cabinet turned to governmental and intergovernmental lenders. The United States extended and increased its loans of the previous year. In February 1974 the IMF provided a standby credit of $1.2 billion. Italy borrowed more money from the EEC in the late spring and in August from the German central bank, the Bundesbank. Its total borrowings that year amounted to $5.9 billion.

The loans had been granted on condition that Italy limit domestic credit expansion and the size of the treasury deficit. Negotiations for the loans provoked a political crisis and the fall of the fourth Rumor government. The PSI was particularly reluctant to support deflationary measures, but had little choice. A fifth Rumor cabinet was formed; it accepted the restrictive loan conditions.

Efforts were made to reduce low-priority imports. On April 30, as a temporary emergency measure, the government required financial deposits from importers of finished goods. These restrictions were a violation of the spirit of both the EEC and GATT, but were technically legal since both the regional and international agencies provided for emergency exceptions. Although Italy's trading partners were unhappy, they had no choice but to accept the *fait accompli.*

Slowly and halfheartedly the government began to apply deflationary measures whose effects would begin to be felt in the last half of 1974. A strong policy of fiscal and monetary stabilization was carried out. Limits were imposed on bank lending and interest rates were raised. By June short-term interest rates went above 20 percent on an annual basis. On June 27 the government increased a wide range of direct and indirect taxes by $5 billion. At the same time it revised the tax collection system to make it both more equitable and more efficient. Grants to local governments and to public and semi-public institutions, such as museums, galleries, and opera houses, were reduced. This cutback was not so much in numbers of jobs as in hours of work.

The effects took time to appear. The rate of inflation, previously above 20 percent, began to decline by the end of 1974. As the deficit in the balance of payments dropped, consequent upon a sharp fall in imports and a slight rise in exports, the lira strengthened. Investments fell. Part-time work increased at the expense of full-time jobs. The full impact of the belt tightening was indicated in 1975 by the first absolute drop in GNP since World War II.

To compensate for the downturn in 1975, economic policy gradually became expansionist. In March the import deposit scheme and bank credit ceilings were terminated. The large Communist advances in the regional elections of June 1975 alarmed the government into more decisive reflation. In August a large spending package was adopted. The money supply was expanded. Interest rates dropped so that by December 1975 the annual rate for short-term bills had fallen to 8 percent. In the last quarter of 1975, at the same time recovery began, the balance of payments worsened rapidly. Foreign exchange reserves were critically low.

A political and economic crisis erupted in the first weeks of January 1976. The two-party DC-PRI Moro cabinet, dependent on support from the PSI, collapsed over the issues of abortion, relations with the PCI, and economic policy. On January 20 when the country had only a caretaker government, a foreign exchange crisis exploded. Between January 20 and the end of May the lira dropped from 688 to almost 900 to the dollar. The foreign exchange market in Italy had been closed for several months. Although the lira made a slight recovery, nevertheless by the end of 1976 it had depreciated about 20 percent over the year. In May the caretaker government revived the import deposit scheme. The following October the new Andreotti one-party DC government then in power instituted a tax on foreign exchange purchases to reduce the run on foreign exchange. At the same time it asked for extensions on repayment of some of the country's foreign debts. Italy applied for a new loan from the European Community. Negotiations for more stand-by credit from the IMF lasted until the following spring.

In addition to the emergency steps already taken, the government introduced a new system of exchange controls and another tight money policy. In the fall a new fiscal policy required more taxes and a rise in utility rates. The expansionist policy adopted earlier, in 1975, to overcome the recession had stimulated a rapid growth of the economy in 1976 (see Table 8.1) but at the price of a continuing high rate of inflation and a devalued currency.

The stop-and-go economic policies followed by successive Italian cabinets in the first half of the 1970s had little effect on the workers in the protected sectors of the Italian economy. Between 1970 and 1976 real wages in industry rose 41 percent, while real gross domestic product grew less than 19 percent. The wage share of net national income grew from 59.5 percent in 1970 to 69.7 percent in 1976. Income per worker rose faster than output per worker. Since prices did not go up as fast as wages, rising unit labor costs accompanied declining profits. Organized labor had demonstrated its power to extract real income increases despite a relatively stagnant economy. Included were substantial improvements in fringe benefits. By the middle 1970s the ratio of fringe benefits to direct wages was higher in Italy than in other OECD countries. Management suffered little from the redistribution of income from profits to wages thanks to governmental support for distressed firms.

The 1972 labor contract renewals set the conditions for an almost 25 percent increase in wages every year between 1973 and 1976. In January 1975 the unions negotiated an agreement with Confindustria to change the indexing formula. Whereas by 1975 the old system increased wages only about half of the consumer price increases, after 1975 the new formula automatically raised wages almost 100 percent of price increases. It also provided for quarterly rather than annual or semiannual indexing. With the wage package completely guaranteed against inflation, union negotiators in the 1975 round of collective bargaining could concentrate on getting even more. They succeeded; in 1976 and 1977 wages rose at an annual rate of 34 percent. The government adopted the 1975 formula for pensions and other social insurance payments. In addition the beneficiaries received one-time adjustments to compensate in part for past slippage in value.

Confindustria endorsed the serious efforts the trade unions made in the early 1970s to improve governmental social programs. The industrialists hoped that more effective programs would reduce government waste and make labor more satisfied, cooperative, and productive. These were vain hopes. Morale in the plants did not improve. There were growing restrictions on management's freedom to manage: to define and assign tasks; to hire, transfer, or lay off; to schedule overtime or multiple shifts; to maintain discipline; to determine products, production rates, and markets.

Key spokesmen of management reemphasized the country's need for efficiently managed and profitable firms. By the end of 1972 Giovanni Agnelli, head of Fiat, was insisting on the necessity for productivity, distinguishing between "productive forces" in business and labor alike and "parasitic groups" who contributed little to the economy for the income they gained.[3] In April 1973 his younger brother Umberto reiterated these themes at a symposium organized by the research group, Il Mulino, of Bologna. At that symposium Giorgio Amendola, a leading Communist, not only noted that workers had to produce but indicated also that his party colleagues realized the effects of the indexing mechanism and wage increases on the economy of the country, and on those Italians who were outside the protected part of that economy.

The unprotected were many: the unemployed, the partially employed, and those working in the submerged economy. Unemployment was especially concentrated among the young. In 1976 14.4 percent of the 15- to 24-year-olds were unemployed. This was one of the highest rates among developed Westernized countries. There were also large numbers of people partially or seasonally employed in both urban and rural work forces.

The submerged economy is composed of illegal unlicensed operations that typically pay lower than standard wages, avoid fringe benefits, and escape taxation. A small submerged economy has always existed in Italy; in the 1970s it grew rapidly as legitimate business sought to escape increasing rigidities and costs of operation.

The high labor costs of big firms reduced their incentive to hire new employees. Industry had two alternatives. One was to increase capital intensity by substituting capital for labor. Fiat, for example, installed a highly automated assembly line process in 1975. The other was to subcontract many processes to small producers and suppliers. The latter were either small, highly advanced, and efficient specialty producers able to pay the high wages and fringe benefits of the legitimate economy, or firms in the submerged economy particularly in labor-intensive fields.

The practice of subcontracting had received passive encouragement from changes in the tax laws. On January 1, 1973, in line with EEC policies Italy substituted the value added tax, *Imposta sul valore aggiunto* (IVA), for the old multiple-stage sales tax, *Imposta generale sul esercizio* (IGE). The IGE had encouraged vertical integration since the tax was paid only when a product or good was sold to a customer, whereas IVA provided no such benefit to concentration.

Based on small artisan-level shops and cottage industries, and located primarily in central and southern Italy, the submerged economy provided jobs for moonlighters and pensioners seeking additional income, for female workers, especially those who could work at home, for workers listed as officially unemployed who collected unemployment compensation simultaneously, and for legal or illegal aliens. The workers gained untaxed income and flexible work schedules based on part-time or cottage labor. Moonlighters and pensioners did not want full-time jobs in the submerged economy. Many housewives, because of their family responsibilities, could not take a full-time job in the legitimate economy even if one were available.[4] Neither could illegal aliens.

The advantage to the employers was obvious; they paid lower than standard wages, and escaped paying fringe benefits and taxes. Some workers, however, had fringe benefits from their regular full-time jobs. Pensioners were protected, also. Housewives whose husbands had regular jobs were covered by those fringe benefits. Public employees at all levels of governmental departments were massively involved in moonlighting, often at the expense of their regular work. The working hours of government employees were from 8:00 a.m. to 2:00 p.m., six days a week, when they came and left on time. They had the afternoons and evenings to moonlight. When required to work by their ministry in the afternoon they had to be paid overtime. Herein lies a partial explanation of the breakdown of public services.

The growth of the submerged economy not only lost tax revenues to the state but also reduced the validity of Italian statistical records. Data collected by the national government's Central Statistical Office, Istituto centrale di statistica (ISTAT), could not include the illegal sectors of the economy. It was obvious that gross national product and national income were higher than the official figures indicated. How much higher was uncertain and could be only a matter of speculation.

Italian agriculture was affected by the spreading submerged economy. In the mid-1970s it was estimated that 35 percent of agricultural production came from the part-time labor of farmers who had full-time jobs outside agriculture. They worked on the farms before or after hours and on weekends. During the planting and harvesting seasons they contributed to growing industrial absenteeism by calling in sick on their regular jobs to work full time on the farm.[5]

After the middle 1960s a process of agricultural consolidation began in Italy as more and more farms were abandoned in the flight to the cities. Although it is true that the efficiency of Italian agriculture increased and farm wages and income rose, the growing non-farm income of rural families made the real improvement in their lot. Work in the expanded cottage industry supplemented wages from urban jobs and farming. By the middle of the 1970s the economic position of rural families was improving significantly in comparison with both their own recent past and the position of working families in industry.

The ups and downs in the economy aggravated the political strife that in turn exacerbated the economic problems. The center-left formula was becoming more unwieldy. Government stability became more difficult to maintain. Alternatives to the basic center-left formula were being urged with increasing insistence, but the political system was not yet ready to consider them.[6]

NOTES

1. Raymond Lubitz, "The Italian Economic Crises of the 1970's," paper presented at the Annual Meeting of the American Political Science Association, Washington, D.C., September 1-4, 1977, pp. 3-5.

2. *Ibid.*, pp. 13-18.

3. See the interview by Agnelli in the weekly newspaper *L'Espresso*, November 19, 1972.

4. Nora Federici, "Il costume," in *Dal '68 a oggi, come siamo e come eravamo*, pp. 286-93.

5. *Ibid.*, p. 292.

6. A conference held at the Casa Italiana, Columbia University, in October 1978 stimulated a number of excellent papers on the economic situation. The following, all mimeographed, may be cited: Gardner Ackley, "Italy in the 1970s: Down the Drain to Bangladesh?"; Pietro Alessandrini, "Structural Aspects of the Italian Economic 'Crisis'"; Marcello Colitti, "Italy in the '70s and '80s: Premises for an Outline of a Forward Looking Industrial Policy"; Raymond Lubitz, "The Italian Economic Crisis"; Cesare Sacchi, "The Response of the Italian Industry to Increasing Structural Constraints."

9

POLITICAL UPHEAVALS

The results of the 1972 parliamentary election made difficulties for both the DC and PSI. The two parties moved farther apart, for the Christian Democrats had emphasized conservative appeals while the Socialists had put forward leftist proposals. Under the circumstances the DC chose to return to the centrist coalitions of the 1950s. Giulio Andreotti, identified at that time as a conservative, organized a cabinet that brought the Liberal Party into the government for the first time since 1957. The Social Democrats joined the DC and the PLI in the cabinet. The Republicans remained outside because of their rivalry with and hostility to the Liberals, but promised to support the coalition as part of the parliamentary majority. The secretary-general of the PLI, Giovanni Malagodi, was appointed to a post critical for economic policy, minister of the treasury. Several prominent Christian Democrats from factions usually considered progressive refused appointments in a cabinet that included Liberals. Their refusal forecast trouble for the government.

Governmental policy emphasized the restoration of law and order, the revival of the economy, and social and educational reforms. In fact economic policy received primary attention. Included in a program of easy public spending were substantial salary increases for high-level bureaucrats in the public service. Compared to persons holding analogous positions in private or public sector firms, the bureaucrats were substantially disadvantaged. Their raises evoked protests from the left parties and the general public. The unions representing lower levels of the public service agitated for similar increases that when granted enlarged the public deficit.

Meanwhile the PSI was rethinking its strategy after its relative

97

electoral failure. Important Socialist factional leaders were fearful that centrism might become firmly reestablished, that the political system could learn to get along without their participation in the majority. At a PSI party congress held from November 8 to 14, 1972, the two factions led by Pietro Nenni and Francesco De Martino, favoring a return to the center-left, obtained 58 percent of the votes. The two opposing factions led by Giacomo Mancini and Riccardo Lombardi received 42 percent. The PSI then expressed a qualified readiness to discuss the possibility of its return to the government with the DC leadership. Andreotti was not eager to seize the opportunity, however; and as the year ended the centrist coalition was still in office.

Over questions unimportant in themselves, dissident Christian Democrats were using their votes to demonstrate their opposition to their own cabinet leadership. The shift in the Socialist position stimulated left-wing Christian Democrats to more aggressive behavior. By March and April 1973 increasing numbers of DC politicians were publicly calling for a return to the center-left coalition. The same spring the government was put in a minority on several secret ballots. In Italian parliamentary procedure the loss of a vote on an important issue is not considered a judgment of no confidence. Rather, a formal motion of no confidence must be introduced and voted upon in a roll call. When on April 12 the harassed prime minister called for a formal vote of confidence the snipers within his own party voted with him and the cabinet was upheld.

Andreotti timed his no confidence motion well. In the first place, he exploited the imminence of his formal visit to the United States, scheduled for the next week. Nobody wanted a government crisis that would cancel the visit in embarrassing circumstances. Furthermore, the Christian Democrats had scheduled a national party congress in early June; even the most disaffected were willing to postpone a cabinet crisis until the conclusion of the congress. Elections of delegates would indicate the relative strength of the numerous factions into which the party was divided. The proceedings of the congress would provide more clues for the formation of a new government.

Andreotti's visit to the United States appeared to reap little beyond the ceremonial benefit of a warm greeting in Washington. Although the trip was pronounced a great success, it did nothing to bolster his position at home. The issue that finally precipitated the cabinet crisis was unrelated to international policy. It was, instead, a struggle over control of the national radio-television monopoly, Radio-televisione italiana (RAI). RAI was dominated by the Fanfani faction of the Christian Democratic Party. Other parties and other factions of the DC had attempted for years to break this domination, but without success. As the DC became less able to control its allies, pressures mounted to distribute access to the monopoly among other political interests. The development of cable television intensified the pressures. Other parties saw opportunities to erode the effects of DC control over RAI through independent cable television. The regional governments also had a direct interest in the issue. Accusing the national network of deliberately ignoring their existence, they hoped that decentralized cable television would give them more visibility. The regional governments also wished to regulate local television stations and collect license fees to bolster their revenues.

The Republican Party wanted to decentralize the national network and open television to private stations. Presumably the coalition partners had come to some understandings. Then in April 1973 Giovanni Gioia, minister of telecommunications and a leader of the Fanfani faction, prevented the operation of a private cable television station in the city of Biella (Piedmont). Ugo La Malfa, head of the Republican Party, accused Gioia of violating the understanding and called for his resignation. Upon Gioia's refusal La Malfa announced in the last week of May that his party no longer supported the government. Andreotti postponed resigning until after the DC congress scheduled for June 6-10.

The radio-television issue remained unresolved until the following year. The Constitutional Court then pronounced the state monopoly illegal, a violation of the constitutional provisions protecting freedom of speech and the press. Nevertheless, it refused to permit the establishment of privately owned networks and did not order the dissolution of the state network. In subsequent years individual private radio and television stations went into operation all over the country. Some were owned in a camouflaged manner by political parties, others by extremist groups, by regional or local governments, and by commercial interests. In a political agreement, control of the two national television channels was apportioned between the Christian Democrats, who retained control over Channel 1, and the Socialists, who obtained domination of Channel 2. Late in 1979 a third, high culture channel began operating.

Delegates to the DC congress in June 1973 had to face two issues, the composition of the next government and the revolt of the next generation of political leaders. Throughout the postwar period the party had been dominated by a group of top leaders who had come to prominence at an early age. Now elderly, they nevertheless refused to give up positions of power. The generation of middle-aged and politically frustrated Christian Democrats made an unsuccessful attempt to take over party leadership. Senior factional leaders, Moro, Fanfani, and Rumor, agreed among themselves to reorganize the party and government. Forlani, a former Fanfani man, was replaced as secretary-general of the DC by Fanfani himself.

They decided to terminate the centrist experiment and return to the center-left. On June 12 Andreotti's cabinet resigned. President Leone assigned to Rumor the task of organizing a new one, excluding the Liberals. In a month Rumor put together a four-party coalition of the center-left consisting of 29 ministers and 57 undersecretaries and including the leaders of almost all the factions of the four parties. Since there are only 20 ministries, nine ministers served without portfolio. Among the ministers were 17 Christian Democrats, six Socialists, four Social Democrats, and two Republicans. Andreotti and Forlani refused cabinet posts as did the two Socialists, Mancini and Lombardi, who had preferred to have their party support the government in parliament without participating in it.

In this fourth Rumor government a troika consisting of Colombo (DC), minister of finance; Giolitti (PSI), minister of the budget; and La Malfa (PRI), minister of the treasury, was set up to make economic policy. Their stated goals were to contain inflation, reinforce the shaky lira, and control public expenditures. Endorsing these goals the PCI announced that it would follow a constructive and responsible opposition.

For some time the Communists had been hinting that they were ready to pursue a domestic policy that would be more pro-government and a foreign policy that would be more pro-Western. Their inclusion in the Italian delegation to the European Parliament since 1969 provided them with the opportunity to take an active role on EEC issues. They tried unsuccessfully to persuade the French Communist Party (PCF) to revise its hostility to the European Community. Although the PCF did consent in 1973 to become part of the French delegation at Strasbourg, it continued its negative behavior in the European Parliament. Also unsuccessfully, the Italian Communists attempted to persuade the left wing of the British Labour Party to drop its anti-EEC stance. More effectively the PCI pursued the improvement of relations with the French Socialist and German Social Democratic Parties. In 1971 it played a useful role in helping Willi Brandt to accomplish his *ost-politik* strategy of reconciliation with East Germany and the Soviet Union. It also sought more friendly relations with other Western European Socialist parties.

By 1972 although anti-NATO slogans were still the standard

stock in trade of the extra-parliamentary left, they had disappeared from Communist rhetoric. At a meeting of the PCI Central Committee in January 1973 Secretary-General Enrico Berlinguer asserted in a discussion of European policy that Europe should be neither anti-Soviet nor anti-U.S. At the same time, however, he vigorously attacked the Italian government for having secretly conceded a nuclear submarine base in Sardinia to the United States. Exposure of the concession brought down the wrath of the left. The Communists were later to say that they did not oppose the base itself, but rather the government's handling of negotiations behind parliament's back.

In the spring of 1973 the PCI responded to a renewal of street violence by intensifying its attack on student demonstrators and extra-parliamentary groups. Behind this strategy lay a fear of the consequences of deterioration of public order for the party and for Italy. The collapse of public order in the years preceding Mussolini's 1922 march on Rome was a history lesson the Communist leaders had learned well. The similarities to the current situation were uncomfortably close. Since 1968-69 the politically moderate public had reacted against the growing violence to give electoral gains to the DC and MSI-DN in 1970-72. Berlinguer, initially favorable to the student movement and inclined to exploit the instability created by the events of 1968-69, changed his strategy in the early 1970s. PCI leaders became convinced that they would be isolated if they followed a strategy of frontal attack on the social structure. In any case, since the late 1940s the PCI had avoided radicalizing politically sensitive situations. The Italian way to socialism was a pessimistic judgment on the success of a revolutionary strategy.

It was apparent in the early 1970s that the DC had a popular base that in all likelihood would remain stable. Years of Communist appeals to the Catholic masses had produced limited results. PCI efforts to provoke a schism between progressive and conservative sections of the DC had failed. If Communists were to avoid political danger, if they were to play a vigorous role in policy making, they would have to come to terms with all of the factions of the DC.[1]

The U.S.-assisted coup d'état in Chile that overthrew the Salvador Allende regime in September crystallized the strategic issue for the Italian left. The extra-parliamentary groups insisted that the fate of Allende proved the impossibility of a peaceful way to socialism; only a revolutionary strategy could be victorious. The PCI leadership thought otherwise. In three articles published in *Rinascita* a few weeks later, Berlinguer reflected on the events in Chile: U.S. intervention was not the key issue. Rather, the radicalization of the situation by extremist elements in Allende's camp had pushed the moderate Center into the arms of the Right. The lesson for Italy was obvious. It too had a large moderate Center that could endorse progressive reforms but that also could be frightened into the arms of militarists or neo-Fascists. To avoid the fate of Chile the anti-Fascist unity during the war and early postwar years had to be restored. An "historic compromise" was required between the Marxist and Catholic camps, between the PCI and the DC as a whole. The Socialist idea of a left alternative to DC rule was rejected. Berlinguer opposed forming a leftist coalition government even if it were to win as much as 51 percent of the votes. It could not survive a frontal attack of the frightened 49 percent and at the same time realize its program of a democratic transformation of society.[2]

The offer of the historic compromise stimulated much discussion and analysis but little immediate action. In line with the trend of the party and with the policy of trade union unity, CGIL engaged in a partial withdrawal from the Soviet-dominated World Federation of Trade Unions (WFTU). It adopted an associate status in the WFTU and a similar one in the European Confederation of Free Trade Unions (ECFTU).[3]

In the fall of 1973 the Rumor government had to deal with double-digit inflation and in the last months of the year with the OPEC oil embargo. The European countries were in a state of disarray in the face of the challenge. Like the others Italy's response was to make the best arrangement for itself while at the same time giving verbal support to U.S. efforts to organize a unified front of consumer countries. In the spring of 1974 the restrictions on the use of private automobiles were relaxed and were completely removed before the beginning of the summer holiday season.

In the fall of 1973 conflict grew between the Republicans and Socialists over fiscal policy and the negotiations for an IMF loan. Committed to a policy of austerity, La Malfa was ready to accept the IMF conditions for restricting credit and reducing budgetary deficits. Giolitti rejected this approach, insisting on an expansionist rather than a deflationary economic policy. The DC was divided between the two viewpoints. The dispute throughout the winter delayed completion of the negotiations. It was a hard winter. In addition to the economic problems there were growing violence, the beginning of a wave of kidnapping for both political and ordinary criminal motives, and spreading rumors of neo-Fascist or military coups.

By early 1974 agitation was mounting to expand the powers of the police to handle growing criminal activity. This issue was added to the economic one to divide the contesting parties further. The DC,

PRI, and PSDI wanted stronger police powers; the PSI and PCI charged that democratic liberties would be threatened. The deadlock on both economic and internal security issues provoked La Malfa's resignation from the government in early February. A week later the press exposed a new scandal: the association of petroleum refiners and distributors, which included public and private firms, Italian and multinational, had been making payoffs for a number of years to all the political parties, in the opposition as well as in the government, in return for favorable legislation and administrative regulations. Some of the current cabinet ministers were personally involved.

Popular indignation required a political response. A bill was quickly introduced to provide public financing for the parties from the national treasury. Contributions from state-controlled firms were forbidden. All the parties except the Liberal Party supported the bill. The law was promulgated on May 2, 1974, granting annual funds to all parties that received more than 2 percent of the vote in parliamentary elections. Exceptions were made in favor of the local parties representing linguistic minorities in the special regions. The money was distributed to the parties in proportion to the size of their vote in the previous parliamentary election. The total distribution would be included in the annual budget passed by parliament. A large part of the public was highly critical of the bill as yet another example of political exploitation of the taxpayers. Few people believed that under-the-table contributions from important interests would end, however illegal.

In short order La Malfa's departure from the cabinet led to the resignation of the Rumor government. On March 6 President Leone asked Rumor to form another government and he was quickly successful. By March 14 the cabinet was in place. It was an almost exact replica of its predecessor, which had resigned two weeks earlier. The same men held the same posts. Only the two Republican ministers were replaced, for the PRI remained outside, even though it agreed to support the cabinet in parliament. Among the first acts of the new cabinet was to abolish the double market for lire that had been introduced in January 1973. Compromising between Republicans and Socialists, the cabinet adopted a deflationary monetary policy and an inflationary fiscal policy.

The immediate question facing the politicians was not economic policy but the divorce issue. The referendum that had been staved off in 1972 by dissolving parliament was again on the agenda. Since another dissolution was inconceivable, the referendum date was set for May 12 and 13. After the divorce bill passed in 1970 the public attitude had veered away from the Catholic position. In September 1971 the Italian Confederation of Catholic University Students endorsed the divorce law, called for the separation of Church and State, and called for the abolition of the Concordat between Italy and the Holy See. It challenged the dogma of papal infallibility in areas of faith and morals and the principle of hierarchy. In October 38 Catholic committees of priests and rebel parishes publicly dissented from the doctrine of church hierarchy and called for a revision of clerical structures. Denouncing the Concordat between Church and State, they characterized the campaign against the divorce law as "clerical-Fascist."

Over the years a succession of public opinion polls indicated that the anti-divorce majority was declining. By spring 1974 the polls indicated that the anti and pro opinions were about evenly matched throughout the general population. The wording of the referendum asked the public if it was for or against repeal of the Fortuna-Baslini law. A "yes" vote was for repeal of the law and therefore against divorce. A "no" vote was against repeal and therefore for divorce.

In the two months prior to the voting, the Church threw all its weight in favor of a yes vote. Dissident priests who opposed the campaign or who supported divorce were suspended from their duties. A small number of Catholic intellectuals who had organized a group called "Catholics for No!" were harassed. The MSI-DN was the only party allied to the DC in the campaign. DC Secretary-General Fanfani converted the question into a party issue by embarking on an anti-Communist crusade to make a pro-divorce position seem a pro-Communist position. As the referendum date approached, both sides became increasingly strident.

The results astonished everyone. The vote was 59 percent in favor of no, 41 percent for yes. Pro-divorce sentiment was 3 to 2. Not even the most acute observers had suspected the degree of secularization of the electorate. The no vote was strongest in the traditional Red Belt regions. The yes vote, while stronger in the DC strongholds of the northeast and south, was still much lower than the vote the DC had received in those areas in the previous parliamentary election of 1972.

The public, recognizing that the law had not destroyed the Italian family, had learned to take divorce in stride. In the previous three years divorces numbered 17,164 in 1971, 31,717 in 1972, and 22,500 in 1973. In those years 76 percent of the divorces were granted to couples who had already been separated over 20 years, and 22 percent to couples separated from ten to 20 years. Only 2 percent of the divorces went to couples separated fewer than ten years. Those families had been destroyed long before the Fortuna-Baslini bill became law.[4]

The referendum was a political defeat for Fanfani. The next month he suffered another in the elections for the Sardinian regional council. The DC vote dropped as the left vote increased. At the end of June a group of dissident Catholics met in Rome to threaten the DC with the creation of a second Catholic political party. Nothing came of it, although a number of individual dissidents migrated to several other parties.

In the meantime the Rumor cabinet had fallen on June 11, the victim of an accumulation of political, economic, and personal strains. It had lasted for three months. Unhappy about the government's acceptance in April of the IMF credit and restrictive fiscal conditions, the PSI was becoming more rigid. The Socialists interpreted the votes of May and June as a signal that the country was moving to the left. They therefore became more demanding. Rumor was tired and simply quit. None of the major DC politicians wanted to succeed him, not Fanfani, not Moro, not Andreotti. President Leone rejected the government's resignation. A few small concessions were made to the PSI to ease credit policy. At the same time certain taxes and controlled prices were raised.* Rumor, head of a weak government, stayed in office because nobody else was willing to accept responsibility for unpopular policies, but the country was left with all of its internal conflicts unresolved.

Despite Fanfani's anti-Communist crusade the PCI did not use the result of the divorce referendum to launch a general attack on the DC. Instead, in early September the party made a public demand to become part of the majority without insisting on direct participation in the cabinet. The Communists announced openly what had been cautiously emerging for a couple of years: they had no objection to Italy's continuing membership in NATO. Giovanni Agnelli, chairman of Fiat and president of Confindustria, reacted immediately to the Communist demand for parliamentary recognition. On September 5 he opposed Communist participation in the majority and rejected PCI assurances about its international commitments, warning of the danger to free and efficient private enterprise. Shortly afterward, U.S. Secretary of State Henry Kissinger publicly disapproved of admitting the Communists to the Italian majority.

The PSI, however, disagreed with both Agnelli and Kissinger. It

---

*The government sets the retail prices of certain items such as gasoline, electric power, bread, and milk.

was cautiously coming to Berlinguer's conclusion that Communist participation was essential if the government were to face the trying conditions of the country effectively. On September 30 Mario Tanassi, secretary-general of the PSDI, attacked the PSI for its intransigence on economic policy and its ambiguity on relations with the PCI. He openly forecast a cabinet crisis and raised the prospect of dissolving parliament. In effect, he was saying that the center-left formula was ending, since without the Socialists that coalition did not have a majority. The other choices were a return to centrism, acceptance of the historic compromise, or new elections. On October 3 the cabinet fell. It was the last one that included the Socialists until 1980.

The Rumor governments of 1974 had not only administered the divorce referendum and managed the law establishing the financing of political parties from public funds. They also put through a constitutional law reducing the minimum voting age for the Chamber of Deputies and for regional and local governments from 21 years to 18 years. (The minimum age for voting for senators was left at 25.) These same governments had also made initial efforts to lessen Italy's overwhelming dependence on imported petroleum. They made the decision to build more nuclear powered electric generating stations; parliament finally adopted a policy to build 12 nuclear-powered facilities. By the end of 1979, however, only two had been constructed and were not yet in operation because of the opposition of the anti-nuclear movement and public concerns about their security in an age of terrorism.

The latest crisis lasted for two months until finally in December 1974 Moro formed a two-party cabinet of Christian Democrats and Republicans with La Malfa as deputy prime minister. It was a minority government dependent on the external support of the Social Democrats and Socialists. Moro's program emphasized an economic policy of retrenchment and sacrifice, and reaffirmed Italy's international commitments. The Communist offer was rejected, although in fact Moro was consulting behind the scenes with the PCI on policy questions.

Two events in Europe made good democrats happy. In April 1974 a revolutionary officers' group overturned the 50-year-old corporatist regime in Portugal. In the summer the military dictatorship in Greece collapsed as a result of its mistakes in Cyprus. The Junta in Athens had encouraged a rebellion of nationalist Greeks in Cyprus only to provoke a Turkish invasion of the island. The Turks were now occupying over 60 percent of Cyprus. Neither the Greek military regime nor its democratic successor nor the United States could get them out. Meanwhile, both Turks and Greeks were angry at the United States, and their commitments to NATO were unreliable. The new Greek government withdrew its troops from NATO and, like France earlier, announced it would participate only in the political alliance, not in the military command structure. It threatened to deny the U.S. Sixth Fleet use of Greek naval bases.

The disputes in the eastern Mediterranean, the uncertainty over Greek and Turkish intentions, made Italy more important to NATO. The Italian government, without Communist objections, promised to make more bases available to the Sixth Fleet if needed. Since the Greeks did not carry out their threat, Italian bases were not used immediately. Berlinguer was proposing a scheme in which all non-Mediterranean powers would withdraw their fleets from the Mediterranean. Inasmuch as the Russians had spent a decade in building up a strong naval position in that sea, it is doubtful that Berlinguer expected the Soviet government to reverse its policies at his request. It appears that he was rationalizing his party's acceptance of the U.S. military presence in the country.

The fall of the Greek military regime relieved the Italian left. The Greek colonels were suspected of having given financial support to neo-Fascist extremist groups in Italy. Moreover, the left feared the Greek regime as an attractive model for Italian military and national police forces. The fall of that regime removed a source of temptation.

These suspicions were not unfounded. In October 1974 Andreotti, then defense minister, consigned to the prosecutor of the republic a dossier on plots for coups d'état that Italian secret military intelligence agents had detected in recent years. High-level military officers were suspected of involvement, and in the late fall General Vito Miceli, the former head of military intelligence, was temporarily jailed on suspicion of participating in some of these plots, or at least of failure to notify his political superiors and to take appropriate action. He was later released when nothing concrete could be proved against him. In the meantime, political commentators suspected Andreotti of having released the information to acquire credit with the left parties for a future try at the position of prime minister.

On April 18, 1974 the Red Brigades came to national attention when they kidnapped the Genoese judge, Mario Sossi. They were an outgrowth of two of the New Left groups, Workers Power (Potere operaio) and Continuous Struggle (Lotta continua). Their leader, Renato Curcio, was believed to have spent some time in Czechoslovakia in 1972, training for violent action. The Czech Communist government hated the PCI intensely; the hatred was reciprocated.

The PCI had welcomed refugees from the destruction of the Prague Spring. The Red Brigades financed themselves by blackmail and bank robberies. They were believed to be linked to terrorist groups in West Germany, France, and the Middle East, and might have been receiving foreign funds. Before 1974 they had carried on propaganda attacks against the political system and had damaged industrial property sporadically. The kidnapping of the judge was an escalation of their strategy.

Other terrorist organizations were quick to react. A neo-Fascist gang, Black Order (Ordine nero), bombed a demonstration in Brescia on May 28, killing six persons and wounding 90. On August 4 the Black Order bombed a Florence-Bologna train as it emerged from a tunnel; 12 people were killed and 48 wounded. The neo-Fascists appeared to seek anonymous victims in crowds; the Red Brigades concentrated on specific targets, choosing most of their victims from the categories of magistrates, political leaders, police officers, business executives, and union leaders.

The Moro cabinet of December 1974 was consequently confronted with a debate on the question of law and order, which began when Oronzo Reale (PRI), the minister of justice, introduced a bill to reinforce the police and expand their powers. The key issue in this early stage of the parliamentary debate was the authority that the bill would give to the police to arrest suspected terrorists and hold them incommunicado for 48 hours. Reflecting their traditional suspicion of the police, the PSI and PCI were firmly opposed. This article was defeated but the debate continued for several months. During the spring, as the election campaign for the regional and local elections scheduled for June gathered momentum, there was an upsurge of terrorist violence. On May 7 parliament passed the Reale bill. It denied bail for extremist crimes, gave new power to the police to arrest suspects, increased police arms and equipment, and strengthened the punishment for attacks on police. The center-left parties supported the bill as did the MSI-DN, although the PSI voted against two of the articles. The PCI voted against the entire bill.

Nevertheless the Communists avoided conflict with the majority on most other issues. At their national party congress in March they reiterated their offer of an historic compromise. They reaffirmed their commitment to the government's pro-Western foreign policy. Events abroad, however, were sabotaging their strategy. In Portugal the Communists were preventing the Christian Democrats from participating in the national elections scheduled for April. The PCI denounced the Portuguese Communists for their Stalinist behavior, but to little good. After the Portuguese Socialist Party led by Mario

Soares won the election in April, the Portuguese Communists who had fared poorly joined extremist elements in the military. The Italian Communist Party and the Spanish Communist Party dissociated themselves from their Portuguese comrades. Nevertheless, the Italian Christian Democrats transferred the Portuguese lesson to their own country and the historic compromise remained more suspect than ever.

Most of the allies of the DC did not follow the DC in this rejection of the Communists. In the spring La Malfa began to allude to the necessity of associating the PCI in the governing process. Although his language was cautious the message was understood. The Socialists were taking a more polemical position against the DC. In response to pressure generated by the women's liberation movement and the tiny Radical Party, Fortuna introduced a liberal abortion bill in parliament with PSI backing. (The bill would have a difficult legislative career for the next three years.) The growing influence of left factions in the Socialist Party and the prospect for increased votes in the forthcoming regional elections stimulated the PSI in its tendency to abandon the center-left policy.

The June elections were the first in which the 18-to-21-year age group would vote. There were over five million new voters since 1972. In economic performance 1975 was the worst year of the decade, and the young were the most affected by unemployment. All the opinion polls forecast a leftward shift. The election results bore out the forecasts. The PCI was the big gainer, jumping 5.1 percent from its 1972 figure to a total of 33.4 percent of the vote. The PSI gained 2.2 percent. The PSDI and PRI had negligible increases. The DC was the big loser, dropping 3.1 percent from 1972. The PLI and the MSI-DN also experienced small declines. The DC vote was down to 35.3 percent of the total, just 1.9 percent higher than the PCI.

Undoubtedly a large number of young voters had opted for the Communists. The PCI interpreted its gains as a vote for reform, not revolution, a confirmation of its current line. The PSI judged its advances to be a reward for its dissociation from the center-left and a signal to continue on the new course. Not all the increases of the two leftist parties came from first-time voters, however. There were also shifts by previous electors from the moderate center and from the MSI-DN.

The significant consequence of the election returns was the major change in the composition of numerous regional and local governments. In addition to holding the three regions of Emilia-Romagna, Tuscany, and Umbria, leftist coalitions now took over the governments of Piedmont and Liguria. Several months later, due to a shift of the small lay parties, a leftist coalition gained power in the region of Lazio. Six of the 20 regions were now governed by coalitions led by the PCI, even when the president of the region was a Socialist. In other regions, for example the Marches, center-left alliances led by the DC became "open" to the leading opposition party, the PCI. This meant that while formally in opposition, the Communists were participating in program and policy formation.

Most of the major cities from Naples northward were taken over by leftist coalitions. Naples, Florence, Genoa, and Turin now had Communist mayors. In Milan a Socialist mayor led the leftist majority. Almost 45 percent of the provinces and a large number of smaller communes were controlled by the popular front.[5] The city of Rome was the principal exception because it did not have a municipal election in 1975. Its election came a year later, and there the popular front won again. The newly elected mayor of Rome was Giulio Carlo Argan, professor of art history at the University of Rome, an independent running on the Communist ticket. The surprisingly large number of offices captured by the PCI put a strain on its bureaucratic resources. The party was quickly forced to promote a new generation of local officials, many of whom had been party members for only a few years, and who had limited experience.

At the national level the election results were interpreted as the electorate's judgment of national party performance. The PSDI shifted to the left to join a number of popular front regional and local governments. To a lesser extent Republican Party politicians did the same. Giovanni Malagodi was forced out of the post of secretary-general of the Liberal Party to be replaced by the more progressive Valerio Zincone. The DC concluded that Fanfani's open hostility to the PCI and his strategy of conflict had produced nothing but losses: the divorce referendum of the previous year, the Sardinian regional election, and now the 1975 regional elections. Fanfani was pushed out as secretary-general. Although Benigno Zaccognini, who replaced him, was not a major factional leader, he was backed by Prime Minister Moro. These two men did not trust the Communists any more than Fanfani had, but they were forced to face the situation in which their allies were in revolt and the PCI was in a stronger position politically than ever before. They therefore maintained Moro's cautious approach to the Communists.

In these circumstances the PCI continued its line of seeking agreements with the DC. Its public advocacy of Eurocommunist principles was intensified and internationalized. On July 12, 1975 the Italian and Spanish Communist Parties issued a joint proclamation of Eurocommunist commitment to parliamentary democracy. The proclamation concluded with a condemnation of the Portuguese Communist Party and a declaration of support for the Portuguese government led by Mario Soares. Four months later, on November 15, Berlinguer and Georges Marchais, secretary-general of the French Communist Party, proclaimed their commitment to democratic socialism. Rejecting Soviet domination of the international workers' movement, they asserted the right of each party to pursue its own way to socialism. They announced that Soviet conditions for a meeting of the Communist parties of both Eastern and Western Europe were unsatisfactory.

During the fall the Italian Communists continued their offers of support to the center-left government. While making it clear that they did not seek entrance into the cabinet immediately, they insisted, however, that the crises of Italian society could not be solved without a serious PCI contribution to their solution. In the meantime the Communists asked to be consulted and to participate in the determination of policy at the national level, as they were already doing at regional and local levels. Moro rejected open PCI support, although he did admit that he was in communication with the Communist opposition. Writers in various Catholic religious periodicals and some bishops warned against any arrangement with the PCI. They admonished individual Catholic politicians against being seduced by Communist offers even when, for example, the PCI was trying to work out a compromise on the proposed abortion bill, a moral issue certain to tear the Catholic world apart.

The Socialists, having concluded that the election results endorsed their leftward swing, were worried that a direct DC-PCI agreement could bypass them and make their participation in any government irrelevant. During the months of October and November pressure built up within the PSI to withdraw its support for the center-left coalition and to go over to the opposition. At the end of the year Secretary-General De Martino announced in the party newspaper *Avanti* that the following week he would recommend to a meeting of the executive bureau of his party that it stop supporting the government. On January 7, 1976, the PSI abandoned its backing of the coalition and the cabinet resigned. The center-left, progressively shakier since 1969, had come to an end.

NOTES

1. See the essay by Sidney Hellman in *Italy at the Polls: The Parliamentary Elections of 1976*, ed. Howard O. Penniman (Washington: American Enterprise Institute for Public Policy Research, 1977).

2. Berlinguer's articles are reprinted in Enrico Berlinguer, *La questione communista* (Rome: Riuniti, 1975).

3. There is an interpretation of this move that sees it as being perfectly in line with the then current Soviet strategy, done with the Soviet government's approval, and not a pro-Western step at all.

4. Alberto Marradi, "Analisi del referendum sul divorzio," *Rivista italiana di scienza politica*, December 1974, pp. 589-644.

5. See the figure in Normal Kogan, "The Italian Communist Party: The Modern Prince at the Crossroads," in *Eurocommunism and Détente*, ed. Rudolf L. Tökés (New York: New York University Press, 1978), p. 88.

10

THE RISE AND FALL
OF THE GRAND COALITION

The Moro cabinet that fell on January 7, 1976 had wrestled with
the recession of 1975. It started the year by cutting costs. Subsidies
to deficitary operations were reduced. For example, in March 1975
the government announced its intention to sell most of the fleet of
trans-Atlantic passenger liners. Regular trans-Atlantic service had
terminated in the spring of 1973, but the government had hoped to
use the large ships for profitable cruises. By 1975 even this hope
vanished. Later in the year the cabinet reversed economic policy and
started to stimulate the economy. The upswing began at the end of
1975 and continued into 1976.

Negotiations at the end of 1975 for the renewal of collective
bargaining agreements proved to be long and hard. Many negotiations, particularly in the important manufacturing and machine tool
industries, were not concluded until the spring of 1976. Part of the
problem was the divided union movement. Since the workers in
manufacturing already had 100 percent indexing, CGIL wanted the
unions to emphasize jobs for the unemployed and job security for
those already working. CISL and the independent unions demanded
all the additional wage increases they could get. Although a compromise was finally reached between the two positions, it was weighted
toward the latter one. The political benefits of the settlements and of
the economic upswing would be gained by successor governments.

In the meantime, the political atmosphere at the turn of the year
was tense. The Communists upbraided the Socialists for pulling
down the cabinet, charging them with risking the safety of the
country. The PSI answered that its purpose was to bring the PCI into
the government openly, the ostensible Communist goal. At this

moment the PCI evidently preferred its arrangement of informal consultations with the DC. It also feared a dissolution of parliament and new elections for which the party was unprepared. The PCI wanted time to consolidate its gains of the previous June. The Socialists, on the contrary, thought new elections would benefit them. They expected to exploit their recent gains.

Just at this time two new scandals, both involving the United States, shook the political establishment. Congressman Otis Pike published an investigating committee report on the CIA, revealing U.S. financing of the Italian center-left political parties in the 1960s, especially the DC. The financing had ended in 1968, but the report noted that in 1970 and 1971 U.S. Ambassador Graham Martin wanted to renew it, concentrating on the Fanfani faction. He also evidently proposed channeling funds to General Vito Miceli, then head of the Italian secret intelligence forces. The report revealed that in 1971 the CIA opposed the ambassador's recommendations. President Nixon and Secretary of State Kissinger turned down the request.

The second scandal exposed bribes given in 1970 to leading Italian politicians by the Lockheed Aircraft Corporation. Suspicion was cast on a former prime minister, Rumor, and on Giovanni Leone, now president of the Republic. More directly involved were former defense ministers Mario Tanassi and Luigi Gui. By 1976 Tanassi was secretary-general of the PSDI and Gui a prominent member of the Moro faction in the DC. Tanassi and Gui were subsequently tried. In 1978 Tanassi was convicted and sentenced to a prison term, the first time in Italian history a cabinet minister was so punished. In 1979 Gui was acquitted.

The scandals in early 1976 made it imperative to organize a new government. After futile attempts to reconstitute a center-left coalition, on February 21 Moro created a one-party DC minority cabinet. It survived in parliament on the affirmative votes of the Christian Democrats and Social Democrats, with the PLI, the PRI, and the PSI abstaining. The Communists and neo-Fascists opposed. The life of this cabinet was unusually short. The following month three parties held their national congresses. The PSI was first. Concluding with resolutions denouncing both the center-left and the historic compromise, the Socialists established the long-range goal of a left alternative as official party policy. In the meantime, they called for an emergency government open to the Communists.

The Social Democratic congress was next. The party was reeling from the recent revelations. Tanassi was removed as secretary-general, and former president Saragat, leading a leftist faction, took control.

The DC began its congress on March 18. The key issue was the competition for secretary-general between Zaccagnini and his predecessor, Forlani. Zaccagnini won a narrow victory. Since he was backed by Moro the result was viewed as a limited endorsement of Moro's policy of progressive dialogue with the left. Moro's prestige was reinforced, but most of Zaccagnini's efforts had to remain concentrated on the continuing struggle with his internal party opposition. There was little time or energy left to work on a program that might have the support of the PSI and PCI.

The issue that precipitated the cabinet crisis had nothing to do with economic policy. Once again the abortion bill was before parliament. In April the DC blocked a liberalization of abortion rights, putting through an amendment to the Fortuna bill when many pro-abortion supporters were absent from the Chamber of Deputies. The amendment restricted the right of abortion to two circumstances only: when the life or health of the mother was in danger, and in case of rape. The Socialists seized the occasion to withdraw their abstention. They wanted new elections. The DC was ready since recent public opinion polls indicated the party was on the upgrade. On May 1 Moro resigned. His government had lasted a little over two months. President Leone dissolved parliament, setting the election date for June 20. The abortion bill was postponed for two more years. It was the second time the legislature was terminated before its normal term expired.

Before the campaign could get under way the region of Friuli in northeastern Italy was hit by a severe earthquake. The event took everyone's mind off electioneering for several weeks. The parties reached a tacit understanding to refrain from campaigning while rescue operations proceeded. When politicking was resumed little more than three weeks remained before the election. The usual increase in terrorist violence associated with an election period supplemented the violence of nature.

The major Communist gains of the previous year had focused attention on the PCI challenge. Public opinion polls in the intervening months revealed growing support for the party. Some showed the PCI equaling if not surpassing DC strength among the electorate. Communist Party membership, which had stabilized in the late 1960s at around 1.6 million party card holders, began to grow again. The party's appeal was strengthened by Berlinguer's address to a congress of the Communist Party of the Soviet Union in Moscow in February. He firmly reiterated the independence of the PCI from the Soviet Union. He reasserted in clear terms the PCI's commitment to a pluralist democratic parliamentary system. What he said was not new; it was where he said it that made the strong impression.

On June 15 Berlinguer gave an interview to the *Corriere della Sera* in which he reiterated party policy on domestic issues but elaborated on foreign policy. Answering a question on NATO he justified the organization on the grounds that its existence was essential to maintain a balance of power upon which the peace of Europe depended. It would be irresponsible to pull Italy out of NATO and undermine the balance. When his interviewer linked NATO to domestic considerations, Berlinguer admitted that the achievement of socialism in liberty in Italy would be more likely behind NATO's shield than without it. "I feel safer on this side."[1] He did not add that PCI concessions on foreign policy were useful as a part of future negotiations with the DC for entry into the government. The interview sparked much interest among political commentators, but it is doubtful that it had a significant impact on the Communist electorate. When a summary of the interview was printed in *L'Unità* this sentence by Berlinguer was omitted. It would have been difficult for many of the PCI faithful to swallow.

The June 20 election produced both expected and unexpected results (see Table 3.1). The Communists advanced on their success of the previous year but not with a gain of similar magnitude. Their increase in the south brought their progress in that part of the country into line with their earlier success elsewhere. The DC recouped its losses of 1975 and returned to its 1972 level. The big loser was the PSI, which had been responsible for the election in the first place. Rather than capitalizing on its gain in the 1975 regional election, it fell back to its 1972 position. The Social Democrats dropped badly, as did the Liberals. Neo-Fascist losses were smaller and the Republicans held their own. Undoubtedly the DC comeback was at the expense of the PSDI and PLI, while MSI losses were distributed between Christian Democrats and Communists. Since the Socialists had argued that it was necessary to bring the PCI into the government in order to face the economic situation effectively, those voters who were persuaded could feel that the best way to achieve this was to vote Communist. The DC, as earlier, emphasized both anti-Communist and progressive reformist themes to regain its position.

Two new arrivals appeared in the parliamentary scene, the Proletarian Democracy alliance, and the Radical Party, with six and four deputies respectively. The first was a coalition of extra-parliamentary groups: Manifesto, Workers' Vanguard, Workers' Power, and the Democratic Party of Proletarian Unity. The second was a libertarian party attractive to younger voters. It emphasized life style and civil rights issues: divorce, abortion, women's liberation, conscientious objection, Third World hunger. Led by a dramatic, theatrical figure, Marco Panella, it used television opportunities to great advantage. It provoked hostility from the PCI because of its competition for similar clienteles, and outrage from the DC because of its offense to traditional Catholic morality. Since it was small and had little organization it concentrated on publicity, shock effect, and the mass media to reach a wider public.

If the DC could feel pleased with its performance, many of its leaders were less so. Rumor, Moro, Andreotti, and other well-known names dropped noticeably in the personal preference votes they received although they were all reelected. In some cases relative unknowns or newcomers got more preference votes than senior leaders. This result indicated a form of protest voting among DC electors not ready to go so far as to abandon the party. It also indicated that party factions and collateral support groups were having difficulty in controlling their followers.

The most important consequence of the 1976 election was to eliminate two kinds of parliamentary combinations. For the first time since 1948 neither a centrist nor a center-right coalition was numerically possible. A traditional lever of DC maneuverability had been removed. For the first time a left alternative was numerically possible, in the Chamber if not in the Senate, if every party from Social Democratic to Proletarian Democracy joined together. If the Liberals were added, recreating the party lineup that supported the divorce law during the referendum, this coalition would have just half the Senate.[2] Since the left alternative was politically unacceptable to the largest of the left parties, the PCI, the only real choices were between some form of center-left or some form of government of national emergency. The DC preferred the former; the Communists pushed for the latter, demanding to become direct participants in a coalition government. Both the U.S. and West German governments publicly intervened to warn the Christian Democrats against admitting the PCI to the cabinet. Chancellor Helmut Schmidt threatened the Italians with a loss of loans if that option were chosen.

Before the issue could be joined, Andreotti, who was asked by President Leone to initiate negotiations, was blocked in his initial soundings by a Socialist crisis. At a meeting of the PSI central committee held the first week of July in Rome the embittered committee members threw out the whole senior leadership group. A number of forty-year-olds took over. Bettino Craxi, a Milanese leader from the former Autonomist faction, became secretary-general. Claudio Signorile of the leftist factions became deputy secretary-general. Enrico Manca represented what was left of the faction of the deposed leader Francesco De Martino. All factions were formally abolished, only to reappear shortly under new labels.

The PSI was in no mood to consider a return to the center-left. The PSDI and PLI were hostile to the DC because of the losses they suffered, which were blamed on the Christian Democrats. Andreotti delayed negotiations while the new parliament organized itself. The novelty was in the organizing process. All the parties of the "constitutional arch," from the PCI on one wing to the Liberals on the other, sat down to bargain over parliamentary offices. When the bargaining was finished, a minor revolution had occurred. The Communists held important posts in the parliamentary hierarchy. Pietro Ingrao, a leading member of the PCI executive bureau, was speaker of the Chamber of Deputies. The PCI obtained four committee chairmanships in the Chamber and three in the Senate, plus a number of deputy chairmanships. It was receiving open recognition of its new position. In addition, PCI experts and technicians benefited from the patronage available in the political system. Under party sponsorship they began to receive appointments to a variety of positions in the state and para-state agencies, as well as in public sector industries.

The DC, however, was far from ready to accept Communists in the cabinet. Its campaign had emphasized anti-Communist themes. Much of its electorate would find PCI participation in the cabinet intolerable. The number of Italians who considered the PCI beyond the pale was declining but those who still did were concentrated to a great extent among Christian Democratic voters. The smaller parties of the former center-left coalition had few or no objections. By 1976 Republicans, Social Democrats, and Socialists were allies of the PCI in a number of municipal and provincial governments. It was apparent that they expected a similar evolution at the national level.

Andreotti needed all his negotiating skill to find a way out of the impasse. The successful formula was that of "non-no confidence." He created once more a one-party minority Christian Democratic cabinet. All the other parties of the constitutional arch abstained: Liberals, Social Democrats, Republicans, Socialists, and Communists. The Missini, Proletarian Democrats, and Radicals opposed. The PCI abstention was determining. If the party had voted with the opposition, the cabinet would not have survived. For the first time since 1947 the Communists were not in opposition. Moro and Andreotti had to struggle with might and main to get disgruntled Christian Democrats to accept the PCI abstention, but Socialist hostility had eliminated the only other choice.

Novelties were not finished. When Andreotti presented his cabinet to the Senate in early August he announced a program that had been constructed in close consultation with the abstaining parties. He did not merely propose what his government intended to accomplish, he publicly set specific dates when particular laws would be put into effect. No previous prime minister had been forced to tie himself down to such a schedule. Most former programs had either dragged on for years or fallen by the wayside.

His program was an emergency one to handle current problems; it was not intended to achieve economic or political reforms. When the politicians returned in September from their summer holidays they had to wrestle with difficult problems. Although the economy was rising from the low point of 1975, the improvement had not reduced the rate of inflation or eliminated the deficit in the balance of payments. Italy was still constrained to borrow to meet foreign debts. Again, negotiations were begun with the International Monetary Fund to obtain standby credits. The discussions were long lasting and difficult, for the IMF was insisting once more on a deflationary policy. As a partial response the government did increase taxes, raise public utility rates, and tighten monetary policy. These steps received the approval of all the parties inside the constitutional arch. The big stumbling block was IMF insistence that the government deficit be significantly reduced. Too many parties with too many constituencies had a stake in continued spending. Agreement was reached only in April 1977. Four hundred fifty million standby drawing rights were granted. In its letter of intent to the IMF the government promised to limit credit expansion, control the size of the public deficit, restrain social security and local government deficits, and increase productivity. It eliminated a few holidays by switching them to Sundays. The successful negotiation of the loan was a signal to other lenders that Italy was creditworthy. A new loan was received from the EEC, and the international banking community was encouraged to look upon Italian borrowers with favor.

In 1976 the Italian economy had resurged strongly from the 1975 recession. Real GNP grew 5.5 percent, the third highest increase of the decade. The rate of inflation remained high, almost 17 percent. The deficit in the balance of payments continued although the size of the deficit was below each of the three preceding years (see Tables 8.1, 8.2, and 8.3). The country was recovering from the economic crisis but no important reforms were instituted that would substitute for stop-and-go policies.

With the Italian public loath to accept any sacrifices, the capacity of the cabinet to restrain government spending was limited. In January 1977 Berlinguer preached the necessity for austerity. His advocacy of belt-tightening and restraint in consumption was addressed to Italians of all social categories, but it was to be expected that his own constituencies might be the more receptive. He was warning the unions, in effect, to exercise restraint in wage demands. The reforms they had been seeking since early in the decade would need further scaling down over an extended time period. He was impressing on local governments, many of them based on popular front coalitions, that their plans for expensive municipal services would have to be postponed.

His words were received glumly. During the early months of 1977 the government tried to persuade the unions to change the indexing formula. At the end of March agreement was reached to make very minor changes in the way cost-of-living adjustments were calculated. It was a face-saving accord to satisfy the IMF, for 100 percent indexing for industrial workers remained basically untouched. The April agreement with the IMF was thus the expression of a policy that did not have public support. The general public was, of course, unaware of its existence.

Reluctantly, the trade unions bowed to the political pressures urging wage restraint. During the course of the year first CGIL and then the other major confederations admitted that wage increases were not an independent variable to be pursued in disregard of other economic considerations. They had to recognize the effects of labor costs on price levels and the profitability of firms. By the end of the year the triple federation CGIL-CISL-UIL adopted a formal policy of wage restraint over and above the untouchable indexing mechanism. The unions accepted the principle of increased labor mobility as a substitute for layoffs. They demanded the right to be consulted and to participate in management decisions, but not to codetermination. In practice neither the workers nor employers demonstrated any propensity to change their usual behavior.

An upturn of both private and political violence in 1977 aggravated the atmosphere of mistrust. Robberies, juvenile delinquency, and particularly kidnappings were increasing. Political violence erupted in two peak periods. In the spring university students rioted again, demonstrating in the centers of the major cities and closing down their universities for days at a time. It was the worst upheaval since 1968-69. These uprisings differed from the previous ones in two respects. First, the students were now armed and policemen were killed. Second, the violence was motivated by the desperation of prospective future unemployment or underemployment. In the late 1960s the demonstrators were optimistic, thinking they could remake the world. In 1977 they were pessimistic, fearful of their personal futures and isolated from a general public preoccupied with its own problems of daily existence.

In the early summer parliament voted increased powers to the police, expanding the right of the police to invade offices or private living quarters, to hold suspects on little or no evidence, and to close down the offices of political groups on the mere suspicion of harboring weapons or supporting terrorism. These revisions of public security laws were supported by all the parties of the constitutional arch, Socialists and Communists included. Just a few years earlier these two parties had fought against the Reale Law, far less drastic in content, calling it a violation of democratic rights and civil liberties. When the police began to use their new powers they were criticized for failure to maintain law and order democratically.

Student and terrorist behavior since the end of the 1960s had introduced a new element into Italian life. Italians are often volatile and excitable, and there have been movements in the squares that toppled governments. In the past, however, killings had been limited, and volatility usually stopped short of bloodshed. In the preceding two centuries Italians had not let political philosophy seriously govern personal conduct and deportment. Now, instead, the student movement imposed ideology on personal attitudes and behavior. Catholic extremists pursued a variety of directions as they felt their Catholic consciences being liberated. Some became secularized; others moved toward new mystical-religious movements inside and outside the Church. Secularized extremists formed a new terrestrial absolute in which faith in violence supplanted other faiths.

The New Left was going through a moral crisis with a consequent escalation of the level of terrorist violence. In part, the crisis was the result of a series of blows to its Third World heroes and models. The death of Che Guevara in Bolivia was one such blow. The overthrow of Allende's regime in Chile was another. Perhaps the collapse of the cultural revolution in China was the blow that the Italian New Left felt most keenly. The mysterious death of Lin Piao, who had theorized the international struggle of the rural periphery against the urban center, the overthrow of the Gang of Four in 1976, the normalization of the Chinese revolution—its domestic and foreign policies moderated and priority given to achieving an industrial society—all had a devastating impact on the Italian extremists. At home the PCI had disappointed them again in choosing not to radicalize the political atmosphere. In reaction the extremists considered it more necessary than ever to destroy industrial society, to take violent terroristic action. Remodeled Marxism, inspired by Marcuse in a utopian and eschatological key, was succeeded by an extreme form of nihilism that required the destruction of everything: the unions, the economic leaders, the entire industrial society, the political parties, and the very state. The main targets of the terrorists were union leaders, business executives, magistrates, police officials, and politicians.[3]

Nihilism emerged most vividly in 1977 among students who called themselves Autonomists and who conducted an open offensive against the PCI. They were the instigators of the spring uprisings in the universities. Their public advocacy of armed action made them auxiliaries of the terrorists and they were a source from which new terrorists could be recruited. They put the earlier extra-parliamentary New Left—Workers' Power, Continuous Struggle, Manifesto, and PDUP—in the embarrassing position of having to support a parliament in which they were present with their six deputies of Proletarian Democracy. Proletarian Democracy was divided over the Autonomists, and the divisions reduced its effectiveness in both parliamentary and extra-parliamentary arenas.

The dramatic German police seizure of a German terrorist-controlled airplane was followed by the suicide in prison of leaders of the Baader-Meinhof gang in the fall of 1977. Italian terrorists reacted violently. The authorities appeared incapable of controlling the terrorist groups in spite of the increased powers they had recently received.

The decline of order shook the fragile unity of the coalition supporting Andreotti's cabinet. After passage of the new police powers the parties decided that a reconfirmation of their agreement was needed. In July this new look produced a broad statement reaffirming the restrictive economic program that was making a number of politicians nervous. The only significant addition was a program of further decentralization. Additional transfers of authority to the regional governments were granted in the area of social welfare. They were given almost complete power to protect regional cultural resources, the environment, and agriculture. National libraries, major museums, and the portion of the nation's artistic patrimony of national importance remained the responsibility of the new Ministry of Cultural Affairs, created in 1975 from the cultural affairs division of the Ministry of Public Instruction. The regions were granted limited funds to do their new jobs. Successive delays, arguments over the machinery of devolution and over the application of the law, meant that by the end of the decade many parts of the transfer were still not operative.

In the field of agriculture the extension of regional powers came by a presidential decree of 1977. The autonomy of the regions was subject to serious de facto limitations, however, because of the EEC's Common Agricultural Program. CAP policies stressed concentration of landholdings and efficiency of production. They promoted large-scale commercial farming and discouraged small landholdings. Christian Democratic politicians, however, favored distributive policies to all agricultural categories, whether or not they were efficient or productive. Small peasant proprietors were an important DC clientele who had to be protected. The regions, consequently, found themselves constrained in their freedom to make farm policy.

On December 1 the parties of the constitutional arch supplemented their domestic policy statement with one on foreign policy. The PCI participated in its drafting, which reaffirmed NATO and the EEC as the cornerstones of Italian foreign policy. A Ministry of Defense White Book published the same year linked defense to foreign policy by tying together in six proposals the Atlantic, European, and Mediterranean aspects of Italy's security:

1. Promote détente;
2. Participate in NATO to maintain the East-West political and military balance of power;
3. Increase military cooperation with European allies, especially in the standardization of weapons;
4. Support UN efforts to promote peace and arms control;
5. Take a leading role to achieve political-military stability in the Mediterranean; and
6. Mobilize political support for military security.[4]

Most of these proposals were beyond Italy's political or economic power. Italians tended to vacillate between two extremes: overvaluation of their abilities to influence foreign affairs, particularly in the Mediterranean area and sporadically in other parts of the world; and fatalistic resignation believing that they could do nothing to save themselves. The myth of Italy's Mediterranean vocation persisted; they still saw Italy as the great mediator between the developed West and the Arab-African world. They justified this role on the basis of their country's geographical location and on its condition as a partially developed, partially underdeveloped nation. They, or at least their diplomats, knew that this role was not taken seriously abroad. Their solution, at least on paper, was to transfer the Mediterranean vocation to Western Europe as a collective entity. The problem was that Western Europe was not a collective entity.

In October 1977 Berlinguer went to Moscow to participate in the sixtieth anniversary celebration of the Bolshevik revolution. He reiterated the Eurocommunist themes he had stated in the Soviet capital the previous February. The consequences were soon felt back in Rome. In November La Malfa precipitated a cabinet crisis by announcing it was time to bring the PCI into a government of national emergency. After waiting a few weeks to observe the various reactions, Berlinguer called for the inclusion of his party in such a government. He threatened to withdraw his party's abstention. With the rug pulled out from under him Andreotti resigned on January 16, 1978. The prime minister told President Leone that Republican, Socialist, and Communist leaders had informed him that he could no longer count on their abstention.

Both conservatives and extremists were horrified at the prospect of PCI inclusion in the cabinet. The issue was mainly symbolic, for Communists were already part of the governing elites. All major policy decisions required clearance with the leaders of the abstaining parties. Inclusion in the cabinet would mean, however, final legitimation of the PCI in the political system. For the extremists this would be the ultimate confirmation of their charge that the PCI had betrayed the revolution and abandoned the proletariat.

As the crisis continued, opposition to a government of national emergency crystallized within DC ranks. It was reinforced by the public intervention of the Carter administration in the form of a U.S. declaration against including the PCI in the new government. The U.S. statement went further, expressing a hope that in the next election Communist strength would decline. PCI leaders resentfully interpreted this statement as a suggestion to the DC to dissolve parliament only a year and a half after the June 1976 election. The PCI had hoped that the Carter administration would follow a more elastic strategy toward Eurocommunism than had been pursued by the previous Republican administrations. Its hopes disappointed, it beat a limited retreat. By the end of January Berlinguer hinted that entry into the cabinet was not absolutely essential. This statement gave Moro, president of the Christian Democratic Party, the leeway he needed for negotiations. It took several weeks for Moro to work out a compromise, and much of his time and effort was directed to persuading his own party to accept it. The arrangement was revealed at the beginning of March. The new cabinet would again be a minority government led by Andreotti. The previously abstaining parties would now become part of the majority in parliament voting for the government. The Liberals opposed admission of the PCI to the majority and returned to the opposition. For the first time since 1947 the Communists were included in the parliamentary majority. The vote of confidence to endorse the new cabinet was scheduled for March 16.

On his way to parliament for the vote Aldo Moro was kidnapped by a band of the Red Brigades. His five police guards were killed. The event stunned the Italian people and the broader Western world. The new cabinet, composed overwhelmingly of the same persons as in the previous government, received an immediate vote of confidence. The kidnappers sent letters to political figures, newspapers, and Moro's family demanding the release from jail of 13 terrorist leaders awaiting trial or sentencing in exchange for the kidnapped leader. The government rejected the blackmail and demanded Moro's release. The political leadership was in a terrible dilemma. To succumb to blackmail exposed other leaders to future kidnapping. It would admit that the life of a political leader was worth saving, but not the lives of policemen, judges, journalists, and businessmen. The terrorist movement would partake in the political process. Yet humanitarian pleas from the victim, his family, and his associates were difficult to resist. Ties of long friendship bound many of the political leaders to their kidnapped colleague.

The government and the parties held firm, backed by the understanding received from the Vatican. The next month, however, Socialist leader Bettino Craxi broke ranks. After some kind of undisclosed contact with unnamed extremists he announced a vague formula that would presumably obtain Moro's release without formally giving in to terrorist demands. To other politicians Craxi's proposals appeared to be a political maneuver to curry support for his party among the extra-parliamentary left and other groups, through a humanitarian gesture. Some of his party associates condemned him for negotiating behind the back of the government, thereby splitting the solidarity of the parties. Craxi's formula, in any case, proved to be in vain.

On May 9, 54 days after the kidnapping, Moro's body was found in the trunk of an automobile abandoned on a street in Rome approximately halfway between the national headquarters of the Christian Democratic and Communist Parties. His family bitterly rejected a state funeral and buried him in the cemetery of a small village where he had a summer home. A few days later a state memorial service was held in Rome, attended by the leaders of all the parties and high representatives of the Holy See.

A terrible period in Italian life had ended. If the Red Brigades hoped to undermine the system, the results contradicted their hopes. The republic was temporarily reinforced. The population as a whole rallied to the support of the state, as did all the important political, economic, and social groups. A few benighted intellectuals advanced the slogan "Neither with the State nor with the terrorists," but the vast majority of them, whatever their criticism of and hostility toward the political order, preferred it to the extremist alternative.

During the crisis cabinet functions were at a standstill. Policy-making had halted, major decisions were postponed, and only routine administration continued. The police and internal intelligence networks had been demonstrated inadequate to their tasks. Francesco Cossiga, minister of the interior, resigned since he bore ultimate political responsibility for the failures of the internal security forces. He was a member of Moro's DC faction.

When political activity resumed a number of items already on the agenda had to be faced. The first was the long-simmering abortion issue, the culmination of a decade of debate and change in the field of family relations. In 1970 the divorce law had been passed; in 1971 the Constitutional Court had declared the old Fascist laws prohibiting the advertising and sale of contraceptives unconstitutional. In 1974 the referendum had upheld the divorce law. In 1975 family legislation was revised. The minimum age to marry for both sexes was set at 18. Equal rights for both husband and wife within the family were established. Illegitimate children were granted equality of status with legitimate ones. Family planning agencies were organized under auspices of the regional governments. Also, in 1975 the Constitutional Court declared unconstitutional some of the articles of an old anti-abortion law that dated from the Fascist period. The Court decision stimulated lay parties to introduce a new pro-abortion bill. The DC had fought off the lay offensive for three years. By 1978 the abortion question could no longer be escaped except by dissolving parliament once more. Social workers estimated that an average of 400,000 illegal abortions took place every year.

The DC was isolated once again, except for the MSI-DN. In the vain hope that concessions might soften resistance to it, the bill was amended to permit conscientious objection from doctors, nurses, midwives, and hospitals not wishing to perform abortions. On June 9 a very liberal abortion bill was passed, almost abortion on demand.[5] The Church immediately began a campaign to sign up as many conscientious objectors as possible. Some intransigent Catholics wanted to circulate petitions for a referendum to repeal the law, but cooler heads, mindful of the results of the divorce referendum, discouraged hasty action.

Referendum time was again on the calendar. The tiny Radical Party, which made a career of using referenda as a political and propaganda weapon, had months earlier gathered sufficient signatures to challenge two laws, the Reale Law extending police powers, and the 1974 law on public financing of political parties. At the time, the PCI and PSI had opposed the Reale legislation as an unconstitutional violation of civil liberties and democratic rights. Subsequent experience with terrorism induced a reversal of their position. On June 12, a little more than one month after Moro's murder, 77 percent of the electorate voted against repeal of the expanded police powers. Almost all the parties opposed repeal of the law on public financing, for obvious reasons. A bare 54 percent of the electorate opposed this repeal, but it was enough to enable the parties to continue feeding at the public trough.

Hardly were the results of the two referenda known when a new crisis hit the country. On June 15 President Leone resigned, six months before the end of his term of office. He was under accusations of earlier tax fraud, of collaboration with key defendants in the Lockheed bribery scandal, perhaps of his own involvement in the scandal. The PCI urged him to resign in the face of these charges of corruption, but it was the pressure put on him by his own DC party that was the culminating factor. The Christian Democrats wanted to avoid a presidential election campaign at the end of the year in such disadvantageous circumstances. Fanfani, presiding officer of the Senate, became interim president of the Republic until parliament elected Leone's successor. On July 9 it took 16 ballots to elect Sandro Pertini, an 82-year-old Socialist and a former speaker of the Chamber of Deputies. The country had faced two major crises and sharp policy clashes in four months. The government had held, the institutions had survived, the political system had shown its resilience.

The parliamentary coalition that backed the cabinet had lost its elan. Its victories were crucial, but negative; it had staved off potential disaster. It had been put together, however, to handle a different national emergency, not the one that erupted in March but the one the country had been experiencing for years: the economic crisis. How critical was the economic situation in 1978? Fortunately for the country, not very critical at all. The deflationary policy of 1977 had reduced imports while exports grew, producing a good surplus in the balance of payments. By the end of 1977 the slow growth of the GNP was speeding up. Agitation by business and labor organizations and by the political parties had induced the cabinet to increase public spending, ignoring its earlier promise to the IMF to keep the government budget under control.

The downfall of the Andreotti cabinet in January 1978 plus the subsequent months of political crises had no effect on an economy that was picking up steam. Italy benefited from an improvement in its terms of trade. Its principal customers were prosperous, particularly the most important one, West Germany. It was buying the raw materials, foodstuffs, and equipment with weak American dollars. Spending soft dollars on imports and earning hard marks from exports, Italy in 1978 had the biggest balance of payments surplus in its history, over $8 billion on current account. As a result, the exchange rate of the lira stabilized against the major trading currencies. The accumulation of foreign exchange reserves enabled the government to repay ahead of schedule an EEC loan of over $1 billion, thereby boosting the country's international credit rating. In September the discount rate was lowered by 1 percent to stimulate investments.

Two encouraging domestic indicators revealed the decline of the rates of inflation and of unemployment. In 1978 the inflation rate was 12 percent, a substantial reduction from the previous year, although still much higher than the low rates in Switzerland, West Germany, and the Netherlands. In central and northern Italy unemployment was disappearing, although it was still present in the south, especially among the young. These brighter conditions were reflected in a consumer buying spree, a return of foreign investors to Italian markets, and a revival of the Milan stock exchange, which had been in the doldrums for most of the decade.

Dark spots remained. The enormous budget deficit of the national government threatened renewed inflationary pressures. *Business Week* reported a survey of 750 of the biggest firms in the world outside the United States, showing that only 7 percent lost money in 1978. Of the 7 percent the Italian record was the worst. Nineteen large Italian firms were included in the survey. Fiat and a few banks made money. The four worst cases were public sector enterprises, ENI plus three IRI companies, Alfa-Romeo (automobiles), Italsider (steel), and Snia Viscosa (artificial fibers). Together they lost more than $1 billion that year.[6] It was clear that the economic spurt and export boom were coming from medium and small firms and from the thriving, submerged economy.

Improving economic conditions were not attributable to major reforms or important policy decisions made by the indirect grand coalition. There was nothing different about the political process even if the Communists were part of the majority. With Moro gone the sectors of the DC never reconciled to Moro's arrangement increased their resistance to the application of his formula of dialogue with the PCI. In the summer of 1978 the Socialists began a short-lived ideological campaign against the Communists, questioning the PCI's commitment to democratic socialism and its true independence from Moscow. Although not repudiating the PSI goal of a left alternative, Craxi postponed it.

The Communist leadership was under attack not only from other parties but also from within its own ranks. It had little to show for its strategy, receiving acceptance neither from the Catholic world as an integral part of domestic society, nor from the larger community of Western nations, nor from the Socialist parties of Western Europe so assiduously courted. For their own domestic reasons these parties had to avoid open acceptance of PCI claims even if they did believe them. The same was true of the U.S. government, which rebuffed all PCI efforts to establish normal ties. Within the PCI Central Committee, among middle- and lower-level activists and party members, the leadership was charged with being too accommodating and submissive to the DC. The electoral successes of 1975 and 1976 had expanded the Communist presence in the political world but achieved little else.

The historic compromise was accepted by most party members but not wholeheartedly nor enthusiastically. For card-carrying Communists the DC and the Catholic world were still the main enemies. After World War II Togliatti had extended the hand of friendship to the Church. The PCI welcomes religious believers to its ranks. Nevertheless, very few party members were believers. Most persisted in their anticlerical sentiments. They swallowed the historic compromise as a step toward the goal they really preferred, a coalition of the left that would push the DC into the opposition.[7] This goal was already realized at local levels in numerous popular front governments. It was aided by the Christian Democratic party, which forbade its local DC organizations to join any government with the PCI.

Party membership had increased during the heady years of voting successes. Card holders rose from 1.6 million to slightly over 1.8 million as the PCI strove to consolidate election victories. The increase was in no degree proportionate to the voting gains, indicating that numerous PCI voters had yet to be converted into strong party identifiers or Marxist militants. The youth vote was particularly volatile. The new members came mainly from middle-class groups and contributed to the extraordinary turnover of local and regional leadership. By the late summer of 1978 public opinion surveys revealed considerable dissatisfaction and unrest among both members and supporters.

In the fall of 1978 the PCI leadership responded to these various pressures. Berlinguer, without abandoning the historic compromise, revised the formulation to make it more elastic, bringing in the possibility of an alternation of majorities. His language turned in a more orthodox direction as he reminded the public that the PCI was a

Marxist-Leninist party. Criticism of the Soviet Union was re-
strained. Communist leaders attacked the DC cabinet for failing to
promote more fundamental reforms. The principal DC contribution
in this direction was the Pandolfi Plan, put forward in 1978 by the
treasury minister Filippo Pandolfi. It was a three-year plan for 1979-
81 calling for:
1. A steady reduction in the rate of inflation;
2. The stabilization of the lira with other West European currencies;
3. An implementation of the 1977 law on industrial reconversion by
   gradually increasing investments to restructure production;
4. A gradual increase in imports as production capacity rose; and
5. The continued growth of exports.

It was not a plan but a statement of propositions. Both the PCI
and PSI rejected Pandolfi's proposals, claiming that they put the
sacrifices on the workers. The DC accused the left of irresponsibility.
Point 2 required collaboration with other West European countries.
That same fall the West German government proposed to its EEC
partners a revived European snake, which would tie the several
currencies to the leading one, the German mark. In 1973 Italy had
stayed out of the first snake but this time Prime Minister Andreotti
was anxious to participate. He feared the political marginalization of
his country if it turned down the opportunity once more. Resistance
was strong from the unions, many business groups, and Paolo Baffi,
governor of the Bank of Italy. They were fearful that a possible
upward revaluation of the lira would threaten Italian exports. To
keep prices and production costs down at home would require a
discipline of work, a restraint on wage demands, an improved level
of efficiency, in other words, an austerity that few believed the
Italians could meet. Britain and Ireland faced the same challenge. To
make acceptance easier the other EEC countries granted Italy,
Ireland, and Britain for an unlimited transition period, a broader
band than was available to the others within which their currencies
could fluctuate. Over Communist protests the Andreotti government
chose to join the new snake. As long as the country was running
surpluses in its balance of payments the threat to the value of the lira
remained moot. The currency agreement was to go into effect on
January 1, 1979. Britain decided not to join. Due to a last minute snag
created by the French, the formal institution of the snake was
postponed to March 15, 1979. In the meantime the countries that
joined conducted themselves as if the snake were in operation.

The PCI did not appreciate these kinds of reforms. By the end of
the year it was hinting it was not afraid to return to the opposition.
In January 1979 its antagonism grew more open. It charged the DC

with reneging on interparty agreements. It then asserted that the existing arrangement was untenable; being in the parliamentary majority was not enough. It wanted direct participation in the cabinet or else it would return to the opposition. On January 12, 1979 the Carter administration in Washington intervened to warn the DC against accepting the PCI into the government. The warning was unnecessary. The PCI knew its demand would be rejected and preferred at this time to return to the opposition. On January 31 the PCI withdrew from the majority. Prime Minister Andreotti submitted his cabinet's resignation to President Pertini, who made the standard request of him to stay on in a caretaker capacity until a new government was formed. The indirect grand coalition had collapsed. Another, and really serious, crisis had begun.

Luckily for the country it did not face an economic crisis at the same time. On the contrary, the economy was booming. The problem was that nobody was sure just how much. In March 1979 the government's Central Statistical Institute admitted openly that its economic and financial data were deficient. The figures did not include the submerged economy. The Institute announced that it would recalculate all its financial reports going back to 1975. It would assume that the submerged economy contributed 10 percent to GNP. The announcement provoked a storm of protest from numerous economists. Many charged that 10 percent was a gross underassumption; the real contribution of the submerged economy was closer to 25 or 30 percent. Others claimed the figures for the whole decade of the 1970s needed recalculating, pointing out that to begin in 1975 would destroy the comparability of pre-1975 and post-1975 reports. Still others claimed that the Institute's figures on the legal part of the economy were inadequate.

The disagreements continued over the question of unemployment rates. Officially, almost 8 percent of the labor force was unemployed. The government figures indicated that three out of four officially unemployed workers were under the age of 30. Most lived in the south. Again, economists and sociologists disputed the validity of these figures. In the fall of 1979 Professor Pasquale Saraceno reported to the Society for the Development of the South (SVIMEZ) that in the south alone the submerged economy was providing 1.1 million jobs. By the late 1970s whatever unemployment there was in the south resembled that in other parts of the country: older men past their prime, housewives looking for supplementary income, school dropouts, university graduates unwilling to take jobs beneath their dignity.

In central and northern Italy there were labor shortages. Craftsmen and artisans were difficult to find because not enough apprentices had obtained the required training and necessary skills. Plumbers, carpenters, electricians, and plasterers were in short supply. In another category workers to do very heavy work or dirty jobs were scarce. As a result, foreigners were moving into these positions, mostly from Third World countries of Africa and Asia. In 1979 an estimated 700,000 to 750,000 illegal aliens worked in Italy, doing the dirty jobs and heavy work that Italians were doing in West Germany, Switzerland, and the Low Countries. Some economists estimated that the real rate of unemployment in the country was at the most 2 percent, almost a condition of full employment.

These circumstances raised another question, just how poor was Italy, how poor was the south? In the north the levels of well-being seemed close to those of the countries of northwestern Europe. The impressive buying spree indicated that inflated prices were not stopping customers. The south was not as well off as the center or north, but how far behind was it? Nobody knew for sure. Between 1970 and 1977 consumption of industrial electric current rose in the south at an average annual rate of 9.6 percent compared with a national average of 4.0 percent. In the fall of 1979 ENEL reported that in the previous two years its sales of industrial electric power had again risen at a faster rate in the south than elsewhere in the country. Decentralization of industry was spreading. Medium-sized and smaller firms were moving, especially down the Adriatic coast from the Marches to Puglia.

The rigidities of the productive process in large enterprises were avoided by the flexible smaller ones. In the final years of the decade many small and medium-scale firms had carried out bold reconversion programs involving significant reductions in cost. They also benefited from a decline in both conflict and absenteeism. Examples could be found in the machine tool industry, the instrumentation industry, and in the private sector of the textile and apparel industries. There appeared to be little future for further expansion of the basic industries that had sparked Italy's second industrial revolution in the postwar years—heavy chemicals, oil refining, steel and automotive vehicles. The future appeared brighter for specialty production—sophisticated chemicals, high-fashion items, advanced mechanical products.

The automobile industry, which had led the Italian industrial explosion, was now falling behind its European competitors. Alfa Romeo suffered severe losses. Its southern subsidiary, Alfa-Sud, was a financial disaster. In 1979 Fiat lost money on its automobile business; its profits as a conglomerate came from its non-automotive operations. It entered the 1980 production year with a large inventory of unsold cars. In the spring of 1980 its chairman, Giovanni Agnelli, forecast a 30 percent cutback of automobile production and large-scale layoffs for the fall. When fall arrived Agnelli's forecast became a reality. The automotive unions struck the Fiat plants for 35 days before a settlement was reached on October 17, 1980. Fiat withdrew its threat of immediate dismissals, but the unions accepted the right of the firm to lay off 23,000 workers during the next three years if circumstances required it. The government promised that unemployment compensation to affected workers would come close to their working wages. The union had been forced, however, to accept the principle of the firm's right to lay off workers when business is bad. Other major industries immediately served notice that they would have to reduce their work forces.

Agnelli had noted in earlier years that Italian auto workers were 35 to 40 percent less efficient than German auto workers; yet they were paid almost as much. At the same time he fought to keep Japanese autos out of the European market, opposing a government-proposed solution to the Alfa-Sud crisis that involved a joint venture agreement with Nissan Motors of Japan. His negative comparison of Italian labor productivity in the auto industry could be matched in the chemical and other industries. In the summer of 1979 Professor Romano Prodi, former minister of industry, generalized the comparison, claiming that for many practically identical items German productivity was 40 percent higher. About half the difference was the result of more hours effectively worked, the other half the result of higher productivity per hour.[8]

The productivity of big firms had been declining throughout the 1970s while labor costs increased. In spite of the fiscalization of some fringe benefits, the remaining benefits paid by the firms were the highest in the EEC as a percentage of labor cost. Between 1968 and 1978 labor costs in Italy increased 450.1 percent while productivity increased 336.5 percent (both in current lire). Of the increase in labor costs, 74.8 percent was due to higher money wages, and 25.2 percent was the result of fewer hours worked. In the negotiations that began in the fall of 1978 for renewal of the collective bargaining agreements, production efficiency was a critical issue, even more than wages. The negotiations extended into 1979 and in the manufacturing industries were not concluded until the summer of that year. During that period strikes and work stoppages were frequent. The wage increases gained in the 1979 contracts over and above the automatic indexing were minor. The unions fought to have the length of the work week reduced without cuts in pay. They joined together with trade union confederations in other EEC countries to make this a continent-wide goal. They wished to avoid worsening any member country's competitive position vis-à-vis the others. The employers agreed in principle to a gradual reduction of the work week if the workers would really work when they were supposed to be on the job. Management also accepted the obligation to inform regional union offices of its overall plans and the prospects for employment. The unions, in turn, accepted the principle of labor mobility, as long as mobility did not mean layoffs. They insisted on being consulted when work assignments, schedules, and locations were rearranged. On both sides there was much dissimulation. Italian employers are not psychologically accustomed to consulting with their employees. The workers, imbued with a traditional Italian attitude of protectiveness toward particular jobs, were certain to resist movement from one department to another, from one location to another. They suspected methodological innovations. In spite of promises by management they feared the loss of jobs.

These were real fears. In the fall of 1979 the Olivetti Office Machines Company announced it would have to lay off up to 3,000 surplus workers. The unions immediately threatened retaliatory action. As of the end of the year the layoffs had not yet taken place. That same fall Fiat fired 69 workers for destruction and violence in the plants. A few days later Alfa Romeo fired four workers in its Milan plant for excessive absenteeism. The union immediately called protest strikes, but few of the workers responded. The fired Fiat workers were well identified as extremist troublemakers who, moreover, were hostile to the unions. The unions called the strikes because they had to go through the motions of being on the side of the proletariat against the bosses. Because Fiat had not specified in detail the acts committed by the dismissed workers, a labor court ordered the firm to restore their jobs. At the end of the year, however, they were still not back in the plants. The whole pattern of events revealed that the leaders of big business had gone on the offensive to restore discipline and efficiency to production.

Unquestionably the union federation of the confederations was in trouble. Internal strains were pulling the confederation apart as the leaders disagreed over the viability of their 1977 commitment to restraint. CGIL, led by Luciano Lama, remained the most moderate of the three confederations, while CISL, led by Pierre Carniti, was the most belligerent in supporting rank-and-file demands. Externally the confederations were losing membership, both to independent unions, which claimed the most of everything for their members, and to no unions as workers moved to rural factories. The unions were strongest in the big plants in the large urban centers. Even where they were present their reduced capacity to control their members meant they failed to limit the damage done by wildcat strikes and by slowdowns. By the fall of 1979 the PSI, which almost always backed the unions in its efforts to gain political supporters, warned the unions that if they could not control unauthorized strikes the government would have to step in.

By comparative standards the organized workers in the protected sectors of the Italian economy had little cause for complaint. From 1975 to 1979 Italian workers gained the second highest increase in real income within the EEC. Only workers of Luxembourg did slightly better. Wages and salaries were particularly high in the fields of fuel and power, credit and insurance, transportation, and communications. This was the case not only in comparison with other fields inside Italy but also in comparison with the same fields in other European countries. Inside Italy there was a substantial narrowing in income gaps between white-collar and blue-collar workers. There was also a notable upward leveling of women's wages to men's wages (in the regular economy), and of less-skilled workers to more-skilled workers. In the fall of 1979 even Luciano Lama admitted that the flattening of the reward ladder was discouraging incentive and productivity. The redistribution of income was not limited to urban workers. By the last half of the 1970s farm labor wages were closer to wages in manufacturing and construction. These changes reduced the gap between countryside and urban centers, between peasants and workers, between North and South.

Table 10.1 reveals which trades and professions gained or lost over the decade. In this table the increase in the cost of living in the 1970s is indicated by an index figure of 1.00.

It is clear that civil service employees at the administrative levels had taken a severe cut in their real incomes. The low morale, the absenteeism, the moonlighting, the inefficiency of public services are partially explained in Table 10.1. Italy had more appropriations unspent than any other country of the EEC because of the slowness of the bureaucracy and the technicalities of bureaucratic requirements. In the fall of 1979 the procurator of the Court of Accounts, an agency similar in some respects to the U.S. General Accounting Office, issued a report denouncing the intolerably low levels of efficiency of the civil service. He condemned the mediocre quality of services rendered, the absenteeism, the spreading laxity that was a rule of life in all sectors of the civil service.

In the spring of 1979 the government had announced a new wage scale for executive-level bureaucrats, military officers, magistrates,

TABLE 10.1:   Consequences of Indexing and Wage Increases in the 1970s for Selected Employee Categories

Category	Ratio of Wage Increases to Cost of Living Rise
Workers in industry and commerce	1.66
Farm laborers	1.65
Transport workers	1.54
White-collar employees in industry	1.39
White-collar employees in commerce	0.83
Professors	0.81
Deputy office managers	0.74
Chief train conductors	0.63
Elementary school teachers	0.63
Section chiefs, public administration	0.51
School principals	0.51
Principal secretaries, public administration	0.42
Executives in the public administration	0.30
Higher executives in the public administration	0.22

Source: *Corriere della Sera,* September 2, 1979.

diplomats, and school administrators. The salary increases were substantial, intended to restore a position that had deteriorated badly. The increases provoked strong protests from the unions that represented the sub-executive levels of the public service. The workers at these levels had received wage increases slightly higher than the cost of living, much better on a relative basis than their superiors. Negotiations with the government over a new contract took all spring and summer. By fall the unions had won a substantial victory. The new agreement gave the lower-level public employees 100 percent indexing revised quarterly, almost identical to the 1975 agreement between the industrial unions and Confindustria. In addition, the government workers obtained a one-time, across-the-board wage increase. The cabinet presented the new agreement as an act of justice to an important segment of the labor force. The government announced that it expected to pay for the increases through more rigorous tax collections. The estimated budget deficit for 1979 was about 16 percent of GNP.

The efficiency of tax collections had improved in the late 1970s but much evasion still remained. The overall tax burden was 5 to 6 percent below the average of other OECD countries. The distribution of tax returns had shifted. In the early 1970s only a third of the returns came from direct taxes, two-thirds from indirect taxes. By the end of 1979 the ratio was around 50-50. It was estimated that 4 million Italians who received incomes paid no taxes at all. Many of these were self-employed. There was an unestimated number who made false declarations, understating their income. A large number of firms, particularly small and medium-sized companies, paid part of their salaries illegally, in cash that never got into official pay envelopes. The bigger the firm, the less this was true. The most honest were the Italian subsidiaries of foreign multinationals, where almost the entire pay appeared in the legal paycheck. Cheating, in other words, was not a behavior restricted to the wealthy.

Foreign firms were coming into Italy as the economy improved, reversing the process of disinvestment that had occurred earlier in the decade. Italy continued to put its external accounts in order. Once again, in 1979 it had a surplus in its balance of payments on current account, although not as large a surplus as the year before. The big jump in petroleum prices imposed by OPEC in the middle of 1979 created a bigger drain on foreign exchange. Nevertheless Italy once more repaid some of its foreign debt earlier than scheduled. Its trading relations with its EEC partners were closer than ever. In 1979 46.5 percent of Italy's foreign trade was with the other eight countries of the EEC. Forty-five percent of its imports came from EEC nations and 48 percent of its exports went to them. West Germany and France, in that order, were Italy's two most important trading partners. Over 60 percent of Italy's foreign trade was with the advanced, developed countries. The Italian demand for imported meat, dairy products, poultry, corn, and wheat had boomed in spite of a doubling of farm production in the postwar period. The doubling took place while the labor force in agriculture declined from 45 percent to under 15 percent. During the same years much agricultural land was abandoned or taken over by spreading urbanism and highways.

In 1979 foreign trade produced over 50 percent of Italy's GNP. The country's main exports were still in the sectors of its traditional strengths: textiles, clothing, shoes, wines, wood furniture—many of which could be manufactured in the submerged economy. It needed from abroad, in addition to basic raw materials, advanced technology, patents, and know-how. These could be acquired through joint ventures or through multinationals. Even the PCI had abandoned its hostility to multinationals. Italy could not compete with other advanced countries by devaluating its currency, as it had done in earlier years. In 1979 the lira was linked to the German mark through the renewed European snake. Nor could it compete on the basis of low-wage labor typical of semideveloped countries. By 1979 its labor force distribution approached that of a postindustrial society: 14.5 percent in agriculture, 37.5 percent in industry, 48.0 percent in tertiary services.[9] The dualism in Italy was less between north and south, or city and country, or capital and labor, than between the protected and the unprotected.

A shift of industry was transferring people from the large urban centers to the smaller cities and towns. From 1975 forward in nine of the 10 largest Italian cities there was more out-migration than in-migration. Florence was the only exception. The decentralization of the economy extended the historic industrial triangle from Genoa, Milan, and Turin to the northeast and center. Regions such as the Veneto, Emilia-Romagna, Tuscany, and the Marches witnessed the growth of flourishing commercial and manufacturing centers. Elsewhere in the country there were expanding pockets of industry: in the provinces south of Rome, in the region surrounding Naples, in the southeastern industrial triangle of Bari-Brindisi-Taranto, and on the east coast of Sicily.

The decade of the 1970s had been a decade of stop-and-go, of floating, or of laissez-faire tempered by public subsidies. In 1978 and 1979 the government would again instruct the banks to form consortia to reorganize the giant chemical firms in order to protect jobs. Nevertheless, on the whole, the decade had been a moderate economic success. In spite of the inflation imported from abroad and aggravated at home, most Italians were better off at the end of the ten years than at the beginning. The submerged economy had absorbed tensions that otherwise would have been acute. There had been a revival of private enterprise as entrepreneurs of small and medium-sized firms demonstrated a remarkable readiness to adapt, and a speed of adaptation, to new conditions. Even some of the big companies had moved to adjust to new circumstances. In some instances the unions collaborated; more often they protested. But in a number of cases these protests were just for the record. The fragmentation of Italian society permitted an exceptional degree of elasticity that enabled it to survive urban disorder, administrative inefficiency, and even terrorism.[10]

But could it survive parliamentary breakdown? The collapse of the informal grand coalition on January 31, 1979, left the country once more with a caretaker government. Prime Minister Andreotti made several efforts to reconstitute the parliamentary majority but failed. The PCI insisted: either inclusion in the cabinet or a return to the opposition. President Pertini called on other political leaders, such as La Malfa, to try to form a government. It was the first time since 1945 that a non-Christian Democrat was asked to make the attempt. Neither La Malfa nor the others succeeded. Two months of stalemate made new elections inevitable. Andreotti organized a minority three-party coalition of the DC, PRI, and PSDI, presented it to parliament, and openly invited a vote of no confidence. He got what he asked for, and on March 31 President Pertini dissolved parliament. It had lasted two and a half years. For the third time in the 1970s the legislature failed to complete its full term. The Christian Democrats were ready for new elections, for the public opinion polls indicated that they were gaining support while the Communists were losing ground. The three-party cabinet continued in a caretaker capacity to administer the coming election, set for June 3. The choice of that date created a fracture between Andreotti and Craxi, the leader of the PSI. The Socialists wanted a later date, after the first popular election of representatives to the European parliament, scheduled for June 10. Craxi expected that a strong showing of other Socialist parties in Western Europe would boost PSI prospects in Italy.

The election campaign was unexciting. Again terrorist activity increased in the attempt to radicalize the atmosphere. The election itself went off without incident. The results (see Table 3.1) produced few surprises. DC losses were minor, but unexpected because pre-election polls had forecast substantial gains. The PSI vote improved marginally, as did the vote for the Social Democrats and Liberals. The big gainer was the Radical Party, the big loser the PCI. The Radicals more than quadrupled their representation in the Chamber of Deputies. Their popular vote for the Chamber increased compared with 1976 from 1.1 to 3.4 percent of the total vote. The Communists dropped from 227 to 201 seats in the Chamber and from 34.4 to 30.4 percent of the total vote. It was the first time since World War II that the PCI vote had declined. The Radicals, led by the theatrical Marco Pannella, attracted young voters from the Communists with a campaign against nuclear power and for unilateral disarmament, the legalization of drugs, and women's liberation. The Communists lost votes all over the country, particularly in the south. Their losses were minor, however, in their historic Red Belt strongholds. They also lost to the increasing numbers of voters who cast blank ballots, and to nonvoters. For the first time turnout in a parliamentary election dropped below 90 percent of the registered voters, in comparison with the 93 to 94 percent turnout in previous elections. A week later Italians voted in the first direct election to the European parliament. The results followed the trend of the previous week. The turnout of 86 percent was the largest of all member countries of the EEC. The Socialist parties of Europe did not do as well as Craxi expected.

Forming a new government took most of the summer. Two types

of political majorities were possible: a cabinet of national emergency or a center-left cabinet. The PCI announced: either inclusion in the cabinet or a return to the opposition. That made the center-left the only alternative, for none of the DC factions was ready to include Communists in the government. They were willing, as in 1978, to accept the PCI as part of the parliamentary majority. A center-left cabinet would require the PSI to reverse every statement it had made since 1975. A number of DC leaders believed, however, that if Craxi were given the premiership the Socialists might be willing. Andreotti's initial efforts to form a new government were vetoed by Craxi, who would not even promise a Socialist abstention. Then President Pertini turned to Craxi and asked him to form a government. Part of the DC leadership was agreeable for it saw an opportunity to split the PSI and the PCI. Most of the DC leaders refused. Their party was four times larger than the Socialist Party in parliament. They had held the premiership uninterruptedly since 1945. After lengthy negotiations a truce cabinet was formed. Led by Francesco Cossiga, the minister of the interior in 1978 who had resigned after the death of Moro, it was a minority government of Christian Democrats, a few Social Democrats and Liberals, plus a very few nonparty experts. It survived on the abstention of Republicans and Socialists. The PCI returned to the opposition.

The new government faced difficult prospects. The rate of inflation, moving upward throughout the first half of the year, spurted when OPEC imposed major price increases in the summer of 1979. Italian consumption of petroleum products continued to grow. In March the government had promised its EEC partners to cut back petroleum usage by 5 percent from the previous year. By the end of the summer it was clear that Italian oil consumption was growing by 5 percent, not declining. Fuel supplies and electric power were tight. The government imposed higher prices on gasoline, on heating and diesel fuel, and on electricity, prices that became effective in the fall. These increases spread through the economy pushing up the inflation rate. When 1979 ended the consumer's price index was 19 percent higher than the previous year.

A succession of caretaker and truce governments was hardly the basis for running a modern society, although there are Italian cynics who maintain that Italy is better off when it has no government. In the fall of 1979 the debate was renewed over institutional reform. The same prescriptions as before were offered: a presidential republic, abolition of proportional representation, and reduction in the number of political parties. In October the PSI called on all the parties to join in the task of institutional reform. It quickly became apparent that no party would countenance any change threatening to its power position. The DC announced it would consider revising its own party rules to institute primaries to choose parliamentary candidates. After a month the discussion petered out. In the meantime the Socialists and Republicans announced that their abstentions had a time limit, the Christian Democratic party congress scheduled for January 1980.

The debate inside the DC in preparation for the congress soon revealed two contrasting positions. By the end of October Andreotti and Zaccagnini were arguing that sooner or later the Communists would have to be brought into the government. Andreotti suggested that the process could begin at local levels. Fanfani and Flaminio Piccoli proposed a renewed center-left coalition with the Socialists. In the meantime, the other parties watched and waited while Cossiga's government struggled with the continuing problem of terrorism and violence.

The courts and the special antiterrorist police squads commanded by the Carabinieri general Carlo Dalla Chiesa had had some successes in catching and convicting terrorists. The previous April a principal intellectual exponent of terrorism, Antonio Negri, professor of political theory at the University of Padua, was arrested and charged with involvement in the murder of Aldo Moro. Although the charge was later dropped he was kept in jail on a variety of other accusations. In May the government assigned army troops to guard public buildings, electrical power stations, and other sensitive installations. This made more police available for the antiterrorist campaign. Private violence was also continuing at a strong pace. In the summer several wealthy vacationers were kidnapped. The Mafia was expanding into parts of the country hitherto immune, on the heels of the spreading traffic in both soft and hard drugs. It was becoming evident that terrorist groups and organized crime were linked.

A different source of violence was reviving in the 1979 clashes in the South Tyrol between German-speaking and Italian-speaking residents. There was a growing self-consciousness of small ethnic groups on the frontiers of Italy and even in the continental boot. It was a development similar to the revived ethnic and regional consciousness in other European countries. In the South Tyrol, in the Val d'Aosta, in Trieste, in Sardinia, Calabria, and elsewhere, linguistic minorities were asserting their presence. Only in the South Tyrol, Val D'Aosta, and Trieste were they numerous enough to elect representatives to parliament. Some were appealing to the EEC to support claims for more autonomy.

In September the Cossiga government attacked the EEC's Common Agriculture Policy. The minister of agriculture charged that in 1978 his country had spent 1,248 billion lire more for food imports from the EEC than if it had purchased the same products from non-EEC countries. He protested once more the discrimination against Mediterranean farm products. His colleague, the minister of the treasury, insisted that Italy's contribution to the EEC budget was too high. Since the United Kingdom shared the same complaints the two countries agreed to cooperate in an effort to change EEC policies. In October the EEC retaliated when its High Commission announced an investigation of Italian government subsidies to public sector firms, asserting that these grants violated antitrust rules of the Common Market.

A more important internal dispute erupted in October when the Italian government accepted the U.S. proposal to upgrade medium-range nuclear missile installation in Europe. Brezhnev's threats and blandishments had been resisted. Italy agreed with West Germany that there was sufficient time to negotiate with the Soviet Union about nuclear parity in Europe before the new missiles would be installed in 1983. All the parties of the constitutional arch except the PCI supported the government's decision, although Craxi found some resistance among his own party leaders. The Communists took a stance equidistant between the Soviet Union and the United States, calling for immediate East-West negotiations before the decision to accept the new missiles was made. They also called on the Soviet Union to halt its installation of medium-range missiles. In essence, their position was similar to that adopted by the Dutch government and to the position of the left wing of the German Social Democratic Party.

The DC congress was postponed until the end of February 1980. At the congress the forces led by Piccoli and Fanfani obtained 56 percent of the delegates to the 44 percent who supported Zaccagnini and Andreotti. A week later the DC national council elected Piccoli the new secretary-general of the party. One week after that the Socialists announced they would vote against the government instead of abstaining. On March 19, 1980, Cossiga presented his cabinet's resignation to Pertini. The president quickly asked him to form another government. In a short time Cossiga created a center-left cabinet of Christian Democrats, Socialists, and Republicans. The PSDI decided to stay out. It was the first majority government in half a decade. Craxi stated that although his party did not repudiate the left alternative, it would have to be postponed to an indefinite future. A Christian Democrat was still prime minister. In the meantime the new center-left government might do better than the old ones of the 1960s.

The Communists were comfortable as the opposition, a role for which they had long experience. Their international posture, however, was not so comfortable. They attacked the Soviet invasion of Afghanistan at the end of 1979. They criticized the arrest of Andrei Sakharov by the Soviet government and his internal banishment to the city of Gorky. They refused to attend a conference of European Communist parties in Paris at the end of April 1980, a conference sponsored by the French and Polish parties with the endorsement of the CPSU. Instead they were actively engaged in meeting with European Socialist parties. In April Berlinguer paid a formal visit to China, concluding his stay with the reestablishment of friendly relations between the two Communist parties. He refused, however, to take sides in the Chinese-Soviet rivalry. At the same time the PCI was attacking the United States for not ratifying the Salt II treaty and for boycotting the Moscow Olympics. It accused President Carter of reviving the Cold War and called on European countries to resist both Soviet and U.S. influence. The balancing act of the Italian Communists on the international scene paralleled their domestic strategy of pursuing reform while at the same time calling themselves a revolutionary party.

As long as the country did not undergo a drastic shift in its internal political balance, the question of where the Communists would finally come down was not critical. The regional elections of June 1980 left the positions of the parties where they had been the previous year. The DC made modest gains over 1979; the PCI held its own. The PSI moved forward and interpreted its improvement as approval by its supporters for the renewed center-left policy. In organizing the new regional, provincial, and municipal administrations, however, it joined again with the PCI in almost all the popular front governments of the previous five years.

The country appeared immobilized in its old condition of stabilized instability. As long as the economy moved forward the prospect for a breakdown of its political system appeared remote. In the first half of 1980 the annual rate of real economic growth approached 6 percent. The rate of inflation was slightly more than 20 percent. Obviously most Italians, with the possible exception of the executives of the Bank of Italy, preferred to stay ahead of inflation, not to control it. The terrorists were not quiescent, however, and in the first four months of 1980 they committed over 20 assassinations. Numerous arrests followed each killing, and repeated unfounded claims were made that a breakthrough in the antiterrorist struggle had been achieved. The worst shock of all was the bombing of the waiting rooms of the Bologna railroad station on August 2. Eighty-four people died and over a hundred were wounded. Presumed neo-Fascist extremists were suspected of this single worst terrorist act in recent Italian history, but concrete evidence was scarce. The public was shocked and indignant. More extensive police powers adopted at the beginning of the year, the appointment of army generals as prefects in some key northern cities, had failed to stop the violence. Some intellectuals feared a future military takeover if order could not be maintained. The danger appeared remote from the minds of most Italians. In the summer more people went off on vacation than ever before. Life went on.

NOTES

1. *Corriere della Sera,* June 15, 1976.

2. Alberto Spreafico, "Analisi dei risultati elettorali del '76," *Quaderni dell' Osservatorio elettorale,* October 1977, p. 152.

3. Lucio Colletti, "Le ideologie," *Dal '68 a oggi* (Bari: Laterza, 1979) pp. 136-38, 147-66.

4. Admiral Franco Micali Baratelli, "Sicurezza e stabilità nel Mediterraneo," mimeographed paper read at the Conference on "Italy and the United States Face the International Order," sponsored by the Italian Society for International Organization, October 19-21, 1978.

5. Nora Federici, "Il Costume," *Dal '68 a oggi* (Bari: Laterza, 1979) pp. 314-15.

6. *Business Week,* July 23, 1979, p. 112.

7. Marzio Barbagli and Piergiorgio Corbetta, "Una tattica e due strategie. Inchiesta sulla base del PCI," *Il Mulino,* November-December 1978, pp. 922-67.

8. *Corriere della Sera,* July 16, 1979.

9. Tullio De Mauro, "La cultura," *Dal '68 a oggi* (Bari: Laterza, 1979) p. 184.

10. Giorgio Ruffolo, "L'Economia," *Dal '68 a oggi* (Bari: Laterza, 1979), pp. 259-65.

11

A TIME OF CHANGE

The cabinet reshuffling in October 1980 recreated the classic four-party center-left of the 1960s. Despite the stabilized instability of the political system, continuing social change could not be forestalled, especially after 1968-69. Neither stop-and-go economic policies nor political stalemate affected the evolution of birth and death rates, levels of education, literacy rates, or patterns of daily living.

Throughout the 1970s the number of marriages per year dropped steadily as more couples dispensed with legalizing their cohabitation. Family composition was changing. At the beginning of the 1970s two-thirds of all families were nuclear families; throughout the decade the extended family gradually continued to dissolve. Increasing numbers of people were living alone. It was estimated that in industrial centers this was the condition of 15 to 20 percent of the population; elsewhere the estimate was of 10 to 12 percent.[1]

Italian birth rates had been falling since 1964, but the rate of decline accelerated in the 1970s. In 1971 the birth rate per thousand people was 16.8. It fell steadily: to 14.8 in 1975, to 13.2 in 1977, and in 1978 the birth rate was down to 12.5 per thousand. In 1978 the birth rate in northern Italy fell below population zero for the first time. The rate in central Italy hovered on the margin, while the southern rate was somewhat above. The entire country was expected to reach population zero by the end of the 1980s.[2] The trend was already apparent in the schools. Elementary school enrollments were beginning to fall, and lower secondary school enrollments were stagnant.

The longevity of the population was increasing. Infant mortality rates were declining. In 1971 deaths before one year of age averaged 28.5 per thousand births. In 1978 the average fell to 16.8 deaths per thousand births. Adults were living longer, too. The decline in the adult death rate was particularly marked in the south. By 1978 the overall death rate was down to 15.2 in the center and north, 17.0 in the islands (Sicily and Sardinia), and 19.5 in the south.[3]

In the late 1970s the average age at death for males was over 70 years, for females over 76 years. By 1979 about 18 percent of the Italians were more than 65 years old. Gradual population growth in the country was due more to increased longevity than to the birth rate. In 1979 the total population was estimated at 57 million. Demographers projected that if present trends continued national population stability would be achieved by 1991. For that year a population of 60 million was forecast.

Increased longevity and reduced infant and adult death rates resulted from changing values and living conditions. Opinion polls revealed that throughout Italy people placed a high value on cleanliness in the home, on indoor plumbing, on refrigerators and washing machines, and on healthful diets. The decline in death rates continued despite inadequate public water and sewer systems and insufficient health and sanitation facilities. Meanwhile food consumption patterns were shifting. People were eating less pasta and bread, fewer fats, sugars, and soft drinks. Consumption of meat, poultry, dairy products, fruits, and vegetables soared. There was a slight decline in per capita consumption of wine, a decline linked at the same time to a more selective choice of types and years.

Regional variations in behavior and values had not disappeared, but were in decline. Especially among the youth the trend was toward national homogenization of behavior and of values. Habits of speech changed however slowly. An optimistic survey made in 1962 had estimated that about 18 percent of the population spoke standard Italian regularly and habitually. The remainder spoke local dialects. By the mid-1970s the proportion who habitually spoke Italian had risen to 25 percent. Another 33 percent spoke Italian when necessary, although they continued to speak dialect at home.

The school is a standard agency of nationalization. Prior to World War II very few Italians had spent much time in school, an important reason for the persistence of dialects. As late as 1957, 90 percent of the population had no more than five years of schooling. In the 1960s and 1970s school attendance leaped upward. The 1971 census revealed that 32 percent of Italians over the age of 14 were without any diploma. Another 44 percent had only the elementary school certificate received at the end of the fifth year. In 14 years the proportion of the people with no more than five years of schooling had fallen from 90 to 76 percent. In 1978 almost 100 percent of elementary-school-age children were attending school. Of them 98 percent went on to the lower secondary school. In 1978, 92.1 percent of the 13- and 14-year-olds were attending the lower secondary school, up from 55.7 percent in 1972-73. Education is compulsory only until age 14, yet by the end of the 1970s over 50 percent of the lower secondary school graduates were going on to the *licei*, scientific, technological, or other specialized schools. The numbers graduating from these upper secondary schools had increased tremendously. In 1967 only 19.6 percent of all 19-year-olds had graduated from an upper secondary school. By 1978 the figure was 41.6 percent. In that year about 30 percent of them entered the universities.[4]

The establishment of the open university admissions policy in 1970 had stimulated a large increase in university enrollments. Throughout the 1970s the government failed to expand the university system sufficiently to accommodate the growing student body. Nor did appropriations for universities keep pace with the rate of monetary inflation. Inadequate funds combined with an exaggerated egalitarian ideology to foment academic disaster. By the late 1970s the number of dropouts was increasing and the overall size of the student body was stabilizing. From 1973 through 1979 only 23.4 percent of university students received degrees; 39.0 percent had given up, while the rest were continuing. For those attending the universities space and opportunities for serious study were inadequate. Enrollments in the major urban universities remained huge. In 1979 over 138,000 students were registered at the University of Rome. In October 1979 the Conference of University Rectors called for the termination of open admissions and the institution of a selection process. The recommendation was politically controversial, certain to stir bitter ideological debate, and unlikely to receive quick action in parliament.

Adult education was promoted by the labor law of 1970. Under union impetus a provision in the law granted workers the right to obtain schooling and specialized training with pay. Beginning with the academic year 1973-74 the regional governments sponsored adult education programs. Most of the courses were instituted to enable participants to obtain the lower secondary school diploma. As many as 30 million people were eligible; yet every year only a few tens of thousands took the courses. Although precise figures are not available, it is certain that much functional illiteracy remained.

Not surprisingly, Italy has one of the lowest proportions of readers in Europe. Surveys taken in the 1950s indicated that 65 percent of the adult population never read a daily newspaper. Among the remaining 35 percent no distinction was made between regular and occasional readers. By 1978 daily newspaper readers had increased to about 53 percent of the adult population. A RAI-TV survey of that year found that while only 23.9 percent of Italians over the age of 15 read a newspaper regularly, 13.2 percent said they read one fairly frequently, and another 16.2 percent said they read one occasionally. The remaining 46.6 percent said they never read one. In 1977, 4.85 million copies of newspapers were sold per day, not even one copy for every 11 inhabitants. This ratio was little better than in the 1950s. Italy can be compared with Switzerland, where one copy is sold for every two inhabitants. The three papers with the largest circulation were the *Corriere della Sera* (Milan), *La Stampa* (Turin), and *L'Unità* (Rome and Milan). The first two were independent, that is, not owned by a political party; the third was the official organ of the Communist Party. The weeklies do better than the dailies. But the 1978 figure of 17 million copies sold weekly in Italy (population 57 million) compared poorly with the 32 million sold in West Germany (population 62 million). Readers of books were also few. In 1978 only 28.2 percent of Italians over age 15 read a book that year. Over 42 percent of all Italian families did not have a single book in the house. This percentage was even higher in the south.[5]

In the 1970s the labor force included more women and included them in more job categories. Government surveys indicated that women composed 26.8 percent of the labor force in 1972 and 32.4 percent in 1978. Undoubtedly these were underestimates since the large numbers of women working in the submerged economy were not counted. In 1977, almost 30 years after the constitution came into force, a law was finally passed imposing equal treatment for women in all careers. Women were beginning to appear in heavy industry in jobs where they had never before been present; they became crane operators and train conductors. The trend was evident in other employment categories as well.

Both internally and internationally the migration of the labor force declined considerably in the 1970s. The reduced demand for workers was caused in part by the economic slowdown in Italy and in northwestern Europe. From 1973 on, more Italians were returning to Italy than were emigrating. Italian workers were the victims of a perverse effect of the Common Market. As citizens of an EEC country they were protected by job rules and employment regulations not available to Balkan, Iberian, or Levantine workers. They had the right to seek employment anywhere in the EEC, but employers in northwestern Europe preferred to hire workers who were more vulnerable, who could be sent home once a contract expired.

The modernizing process in Italy resembled the process in other countries of the Western World. The accumulation of durable consumer goods had effects in Italy similar to those of its northwestern European neighbors. Mass acquisitions of refrigerators, washing machines, and modern kitchens and bathrooms came quickly after the diffusion of electric power networks throughout the country. The rapid spread of radio and television and of the family automobile served to destroy the historic isolation of the various regions. The government was losing its domination over the listening and viewing public. In the last half of the 1970s private radio and television stations made major inroads on the audiences formerly monopolized by the government-controlled networks. Surveys indicated that by the end of the decade 40 percent of the total radio audience was listening to private radio stations. By 1979 there was one automobile for every 3.4 inhabitants of the nation, plus 5 million motorcycles and motorbikes. People were traveling; the boom in the tourist and vacation industry was not just the result of the foreign tourist invasion of the country.

The spreading secularization of society reflected cultural as well as physical mobility. Ways of looking at religion were also in flux. Church attendance continued to decline. Among those people who were getting married the number married only in civil ceremonies rose—from less than 2 percent of all marriages in the immediate postwar period to about 12 percent by the end of the 1970s. Interest in religion took a variety of forms; exploration of oriental mystical movements, activities by evangelical groups such as Jehovah's Witnesses, new types of Catholic communities and practices, and deviations from the institutional, hierarchical Church. In all cases these new directions were taken by small groups who were, however, sufficiently numerous to be subjects of interest to the press. At the same time the Church was recouping some of its influence. Since the split in the early 1970s between ACLI and the Church hierarchy, there had been a rethinking and reconciliation between the two, though ACLI still avoided political formulas and alliances. Discussions between the Church and the government concerning revision of the Concordat moved slowly. The deaths of two popes created delays. The Holy See posed no objection to eliminating the designation of the Roman Catholic Church as the official state church. It was ready to give up the description of Rome as a sacred city; after all, the municipality had a Communist mayor. But no agreement could be reached on the question of religious teaching in the public schools, nor could the dispute over the taxation of nonreligious Church property be resolved. Secular groups who wanted to exclude only religious structures from property taxation would not define Catholic schools or hospitals as religious structures. Consequently, negotiations continued into the 1980s.

Negative effects of modernization were spreading. Several problems of contemporary urban life afflicted the nation, with the authorities apparently incapable of bringing them under control. Nonpolitical crimes proliferated. In 1968 records showed 16.7 criminal acts per 1,000 inhabitants. In the next decade the murder rate doubled, thefts more than tripled, and extortion and kidnapping increased 600 percent. These increases resulted partly from better statistics and more publicity and partly from a genuine increase in criminal behavior. There was a big increase in the 1970s of the consumption of both soft and hard drugs. The streets of the cities were not as safe as in the past; apartment dwellers barricaded themselves behind multilocked doors.

Resource conservation and antipollution programs existed on paper but were neglected in fact. Fertile land was disappearing and forests were few. The great floods of the Arno River and Venice Lagoon in 1966 produced little subsequent action to prevent repetitions. In 1979 the northwestern regions of Lombardy, Piedmont, and Liguria were flooded. In 1976 parliament passed a law to control pollution and to repurify water. In 1977 Italy entered into treaty agreements with other countries of the Mediterranean basin to stop polluting the waters and continental shelf of the Mediterranean Sea. By 1979 parliament suspended the 1976 law because so little had been done by municipalities, provinces, regions, and private and public firms to control pollution and to repair earlier damage. The response of all these organizations was that they lacked the money. In 1979 many beaches were closed to bathers because of polluted waters. The failure to invest in conservation and antipollution measures threatened economic growth as well as the livability of city and countryside.

The trade unions had made social reforms a primary target of political action in the 1970s. High priority among these reforms was assigned to more and improved housing, especially public housing. Although Italy needed 400,000 new dwelling units a year for many years to meet a stored-up demand, at the end of the decade only 150,000 to 160,000 were being built annually. In 1979 public housing construction was only 3 percent of total housing construction. Funds for public housing are scarce when the government has a huge budget deficit and gives a higher priority to subsidizing unprofitable industries.

Italy was living through developments and problems that were the same as in other advanced societies. Its population, like other populations, was asserting what Daniel Bell has called the "revolution of rising entitlements." This revolution is most successful when more entitlements can be financed out of economic growth. In the 1970s economic growth was present though spotty. The rate of inflation was one of the highest among the advanced countries, but a good share of the population was able to keep ahead of it. For many families this required two or more incomes, a requirement not unique to Italy. The submerged economy helped pull the nation through some difficult years. Could it continue to do so?

This was both a moral and an economic question. Although the government was losing tax revenues from illegal employers and their workers, the losses were partially offset since the public treasury did not have to support a larger burden of welfare expenditures. But the workers in the submerged economy were exploited and without protection. The rigidities of the protected labor market sector contributed to the growth of the unprotected sector, since an unemployed worker could always argue that exploited work was better than no work.

The economy as a whole had become increasingly dependent on foreign trade and therefore increasingly vulnerable to upheavals and disruptions in that trade. As foreign protectionist pressures rose, the Italians faced a potential loss of markets. As high rates of domestic inflation pushed prices and costs upward Italian producers became vulnerable to foreign competition not only in their own markets but even more so in external markets. In the fall of 1980 the export boom was in danger. Some large firms were pressuring the government to abandon the snake entered into just the year before, to devalue the lira in order to keep the firms competitive abroad. Other firms, and critical economists as well, suggested as an alternative to devaluation that the government assume more of workers' fringe benefits now paid by employers: for devaluation would feed inflation at home and its stimulus to exports could be only temporary. Surpluses in the balance of payments on current account were replaced by deficits. The Iraq-Iran war threatened Italy with another dramatic increase in petroleum prices. The government budgetary deficit was rising significantly. The lira was weakening. Once again the economy was endangered.

The political system had muddled through more than a decade of expediency. No legislature after 1968 had completed its full five-year term of office. The 1968 legislature lasted four years, the 1972 legislature four years, and the 1976 legislature three years. Throughout the 1970s no stable political formula underlay the successive cabinets. Most goverments were either minority governments, care-taker governments, or truce governments. Sometimes they had majority support in parliament; at other times they depended on abstentions. It is true that even the occasional majority government rarely accomplished more than the others. And the period was not devoid of some important legislation: the labor law of 1970, the establishment of governments for the regular regions in 1970, the divorce law of 1970, the reduction of the voting age for the Chamber of Deputies in 1974, public financing of political parties in 1974, the abortion law of 1978, and the various internal security laws of which the Reale Law is best known. Additional legislation to improve security brought few results, for both private and political violence continued to increase, and crime continued to spread. The growing sense of insecurity in the large urban centers reflected not only the inadequacies of the various police forces but also the fragility of social structures.

The hope that decentralization would bind the population more closely to the political system was disappointed. The financial dependence of the regional and local governments on the national government and the many functions they were mandated to perform effectively undercut decentralization and left them little autonomy. None of the regions had truly formulated a regional development program on the basis of which it could ask the central government for necessary resources. There was no framework for making regional policy decisions.

In the name of participatory democracy parliament passed legislation in 1976 and 1977 creating neighborhood committees and school committees of students, teachers, parents, and administrators that had no power. They were advisory; in one case to the municipal governments, in the other to the provincial superintendents of schools, who in turn were officials of the Ministry of Public Instruction. These community organizations fell almost completely under the domination of the left and extra-parliamentary left parties. Under party manipulation they drove out participants from other sectors of the population. The experiment was a failure.

No Italian government had found formulas to control inflation, stimulate steady economic growth, or distribute the financial rewards in a politically equitable manner. Neither had other governments, but many others were less vulnerable to the economic hurricanes circulating throughout the world. The revolution of rising entitlements prevented any government from imposing a policy of personal austerity. In Italy, every social group was certain that it alone would pay the price of retrenchment while all the others would continue to take care of themselves. The Christian Democrats and Socialists were unwilling to deny almost any claimant a share of the public treasury. The Republicans and Communists talked about austerity and fiscal responsibility. The Republicans, however, were a tiny party without much political impact. The Communists retreated every time a subsidy was requested to preserve jobs. In August 1979 Berlinguer reiterated that austerity was not to be borne by wage earners alone but must be endured by all social groups. While it is true that the unprotected—the unemployed, the aliens, the underemployed—were well acquainted with austerity in spite of the existence of the welfare state, Italian society as a whole lacked sufficient cohesion to integrate its social groups in any policy of sacrifice.

The leftist formula of democratic programming was nothing more than a variant on the existing mixed economy of limited laissez-faire supplemented by government subsidies. By the late 1970s the PCI had little taste for more government nationalization of industry and no illusions about the inadequacies of a command economy.[6] The DC policy of buying and holding the support of clientelistic groups through the distribution of favors depended on having available resources. The slower growth of the economy in the 1970s reduced but did not eliminate these resources.

A different approach to the nation's economic problems would have to come from a political coalition other than the one centered on Christian Democracy. In the early 1970s the Socialists had proposed the left alternative as the long-run goal. It was the only possible alternative within the framework of the existing political system. The Communists had instead opted for the historic compromise, involving a long-run agreement with the DC coupled with a hope of changing the nature of Christian Democracy. By 1979 the PCI was thinking more favorably of the left alternative. Whether such an alternative would really postulate a different kind of economic order and attempt to implement it remained speculative. Descriptions of the economic content of the system Communists called democratic socialism were vague and abstract. Communist leaders really did not know what democratic socialism would be like. All they knew was that it would be different from any socialist system in existence.

In the spring of 1980 the PSI returned to the formula of the center-left. When the cabinet was reshuffled in October 1980 the Social Democrats were included in the governing coalition, thereby recreating the four-party alignment of Christian Democratic, Socialist, Social Democratic, and Republican parties. In the same month the Socialists and Social Democrats announced their agreement to consult, to collaborate, and to establish joint positions on policy although they denied any intention of reuniting in the immediate future. The two parties affirmed their clear adherence to the values of "Western Socialism." Whatever these values may be, since World War II they have not included open collaboration with Communists except in France and Italy. With this agreement Craxi not only undercut the left wing of his own party but also made it clear that the Socialists were abandoning the left alternative at the national level when the Communists had become more interested in it. The PCI was in a cul-de-sac; neither the historic compromise nor the left alternative was realizable.

But the left alternative flourished at sub-national levels. As a result of regional and local elections in June 1980 almost all of the popular front governments were reconstituted in the regions, provinces, and municipalities where they were functioning already. Social Democrats and Republicans participated in some of these governments. That the open historic compromise did not replace the left alternative at these levels was owing to DC refusal to allow its local units to participate in these coalitions, not to exclusionary policies followed by Communists and Socialists. Though the DC would not govern together with the PCI at any level of government, it was ready to invite Communist collaboration—a necessary condition to maintaining what social peace there was in the country. In the 1960s the old center-left had been promoted as a way to isolate and undercut the PCI. The new center-left of 1980 had no such aspiration. The DC, in any case, expected to continue its leading role in national affairs, reasonably confident that no other party or combination of parties was able or willing to challenge its leadership.

The absence of a credible opposition to the DC created what some commentators called the "blocked political system." The blockage was blamed as a major cause of the extremist strategy of terror in the 1970s. No clear-cut choices could emerge to reduce the tension. There were no decisive victories for either a democratic left or a democratic right.[7] That the extremists of the Red Brigades or Front Line would have accepted the policies of the only feasible alternative centered on the Communist Party is highly doubtful. In spite of their libertarian Marxist doctrines, their behavior and their language were more Fascist than anything else. The PCI accused the extraparliamentary left, especially the extremists of the autonomist university-student movement, of behaving like Fascists. In cautious academic language a scholar of the Fascist period wrote:

As the Fascist period recedes in time, many attitudes which it

favoured are becoming fashionable again: we have only to think of
the spawning of irrationalism, voluntarism, anti-intellectualism,
the exaltation of youth over maturity, spontaneity over organization, of actions which are dictated by emotional frustration over
those which are based on rational analysis.[8]

Whether or not there is an alternation in the roles of government
and opposition, the leading parties in an open political system must
establish understandings among themselves about the rules of the
political game. The center-left was one kind of understanding, the
indirect grand coalition another. The mutual decision to concede
each other's role as leader of the government or the opposition, each
with its privileges, is yet another understanding and one the DC and
PCI have been accused of making tacitly. All of these game plans
require compromises that must be arranged by the political leadership.

The political leadership was hampered in the management of the
political process by continuing residual differences of values and
attitudes rooted within their followers. Although the direct intervention of the Church hierarchy in political affairs had declined, many
of the DC electoral supporters still held the traditional values of
family, doctrinaire authority, intolerance of differences, and confor-
mity to the standard criteria of respectability. The PCI, on the other
hand, had to manage an important sector of its rank and file that was
still tied to the maximalist revolutionary tradition, to residual
dogmas, and to millenarian visions of charismatic forces capable of
launching revolutions. There remained a continuing suspicion of the
Church and hostility to the Christian Democrats. Many Communist
and Socialist supporters shared some of the positions of the extra-
parliamentary left. Nevertheless a significant minority of left-wing
voters espoused conservative values, particularly on life-style issues
such as personal behavior, dress, parental authority, and stability of
institutions.[9] Berlinguer was justified in his fears that radicalizing
the political atmosphere in Italy would drive large numbers of
moderates into the hands of the right, for he also risked the same
threat from a part of his own following.

The Communist Party's Italian way to socialism had to operate
within these limiting contradictions. It accepted the alternation of
majorities in the country but rejected alternation inside the party. It
accepted a pluralism of values, religions, and philosophies, and
asserted the hegemony of the proletariat, insisting that these were
not incompatible concepts.[10] It wavered between minimizing and
emphasizing its Marxist-Leninist origins and remained ambiguous

in its relations with the Soviet Union. The party wanted to get the political and economic system in Italy functioning again. The leaders did not believe "so much the worse, so much the better." Yet they insisted that the party's goal was not to reform the system but to transform it.

In 1964 Giorgio Amendola called for a new, unified party of the working class, neither communist in the orthodox sense, nor social democratic. At the time he hoped that Socialists and Social Democrats would join Communists in the creation of this new party.[11] His hopes were unrealized, but in subsequent years his own party evolved in the direction he had projected. But was the evolution enough? For some of its supporters it was too much; for sectors of the Socialist electorate the PCI had hoped but had failed to reach, it was not enough. These Socialists wanted to see the PCI social-democratized and to see a clear-cut split between it and the Soviet Union. The PCI would not, or could not, take these steps so in 1979 it lost votes from among those who thought it had gone too far, and failed to gain votes from those it had hoped to attract. At the same time most Communist leaders rejected even a partial return to orthodoxy. The PCI was Eurocommunist, they believed, because Eurocommunism was the only kind of communism relevant to advanced modern societies. Italy was such a society and would remain one.

No such debates over identity disturbed the sleep of Christian Democracy. Its leaders wrangled over power and possessions. Whatever clashes, and they were many, marked the rivalries of the factions, they were no longer motivated by distinctions of program. Between those rejecting and those accepting the eventual inclusion of the PCI in a government, policy differences centered on the costs to the DC of such a prospect. There were also differences of opinion between those who felt Italy could be governed without the Communists but not against them, and those who believed the country could also be governed against the PCI. In the Communist Party there were differences between those who thought that a left alternative might be formed in the future without the DC, but not against the DC, and those who still chose an historic compromise. In all cases, however, these debates and the political developments that produced them revealed the incomplete integration of the PCI into the Italian political system.

Moreover, neither Eurocommunist nor Social Catholic doctrines were adequate for a modern consumer society. The solidity of electoral support for the parties was beginning to erode. In the 1979 parliamentary election the voter turnout fell to just below 90 percent of the eligible electorate for the first time. The turnout in the 1980 regional elections dropped to 88.5 percent, the lowest in the entire postwar period. Furthermore, an increasing number of those who did vote cast invalid or blank ballots. Although these developments were interpreted by politicians and political analysts as a protest against the parties and the political system, they must be understood in context. Italy still has one of the highest voter turnouts in the modern democratic world. However much the parties lagged at the ideological level, they remained skillful at the electoral level.

The electorate manifested a growing fluidity. The south had always been more politically volatile than other parts of the country, but fluidity in party identification was extending to other zones over and above any political influence attributable to southern migration. The electorate was becoming gradually freer of dogmatic or sub-cultural origins. Voters' electoral choices were reflecting more weight given to judgments on policies and performance and less emphasis on tradition and identity. The change was hidden by compensating shifts in voting choices that resulted in the overall stability of the final election returns, but nevertheless the change in voting behavior was there.

Even so, high percentages of voters and overall stability of the vote could not hide popular discontent. The masses of the people and educated opinion leaders alike believed that the political system functioned disgracefully, producing frustration, disaffection, and impotence.[12] Public opinion polls revealed the disillusion with political parties, which was particularly marked among the youth. Another indication of popular dismay was the response to the 1978 referendum on the law providing for the public financing of the political parties; 46 percent voted against the law. A general hostility to the parties buttressed a widespread belief in the existence of a fracture between the political elites and the population as a whole. Even supporters of the two major parties, the DC and the PCI, held this opinion. People had daily reminders of governmental malfunctioning in the inadequacies of the postal system and in the hours spent waiting in the post offices, the banks, and administrative offices. Throughout most of the 1970s coins were lacking to make small change; hard candies and postage stamps served as substitutes for 5-, 10-, and even 50-lire pieces. By 1979 the overall situation was improving but had not yet been resolved. The people's patience with the low levels of public service was remarkable.

In spite of double-digit inflation and stop-and-go economic policies the vast majority of the population was materially far better off than ever before, but industry in Italy was not. Even though the vitality and dynamism of the small and medium-sized firms in the private sector was striking, nevertheless the same could not be said for large industries, either public or private. Their pessimistic prognosis of their future in Italy led them to shift their investments during the 1970s to foreign countries.

During the same decade organized labor's power reached its apex, in the workplace and in its influence on social policy. By the end of the period it appeared that this power was beginning to decline. Management was again asserting its right to manage; to modify production methods that might require workers to shift jobs or to use new techniques; to fire for excessive absenteeism; to lay workers off when business declined. At the same time the government was imposing austerity programs, increasing taxes and prices, while squeezing consumer standards of living.

Discipline might be returning in the factories but people were more free in their private and social lives than ever before. The changing condition of women was one example of the increased personal liberty. The heightened informality of dress and social intercourse was another. In a contrary direction the population in the large urban centers became afraid of being out on the streets at night. The extension of police powers in the antiterrorist campaign was a potential threat to civil rights and to democracy, although on the whole there had been few abuses of these powers. Postwar governmental policies had produced many positive results, yet these gains had done little to strengthen national political identity.

There was a pervasive sense of discontent that went beyond the political sphere. Italians were not happy with their lives as a whole, in spite of the real improvements in their conditions. A cross-national survey taken in 1977 by Gallup International Research Institutes revealed widely differing responses by Western populations to questions concerning life satisfactions. In the United States 69 percent of the citizens were highly satisfied with life as a whole, as were 67 percent of the Danes, 59 percent of the Irish, 57 percent of the Dutch, 51 percent of the Belgians, 50 percent of the British, 41 percent of the West Germans, and 26 percent of the French. Only 17 percent of the Italians were highly satisfied with life as a whole.[13]

The political system deserves part of the blame for the low level of satisfaction with life. But it also deserves part of the credit for having raised the expectations and hopes of a people many of whom had never before enjoyed the luxury of aspiration. That Italians were dissatisfied with the everyday realities of life indicated the new criteria that they had adopted in contemporary times. Unrealized higher popular expectations could be potentially dangerous, but the people as a whole were demonstrating remarkable patience. The reradicalization of Italy after 1968 proved to be quite limited in real political impact or in penetration of most of the population.

The political leaders of the large parties had for the most part avoided polarizing slogans and intransigent behavior. They were rivals and competitors, but they had resisted the urgings of extremist supporters to decimate opponents. As a result most of the significant political and interest group elites had developed a real stake in the parliamentary republic. Thus the government survived, even if it did not govern very well.

The political system and the political leadership enjoyed little esteem, but when the system was struck at its very heart by the kidnapping and assassination of Aldo Moro the people rallied to it. They backed the state, not its enemies nor those who were indifferent. Perhaps their sense of national political identity was not as weak as their responses to pollsters indicated. Perhaps there was more consensus and less fragmentation than they expressed. The people had survived difficult tests with remarkable resilience. They continued to be Italy's real heroes.

NOTES

1. Nora Federici, "Il costume," pp. 277-81.
2. *Ibid.*, pp. 274-75.
3. Tullio De Mauro, "La cultura," p. 181.
4. *Ibid.*, pp. 191-200.
5. *Ibid.*, pp. 207-10, 215-16.
6. Lucio Libertini, "The Problem of the PCI," p. 3, mimeographed paper presented at the conference on "Italy and Eurocommunism, Western Europe at the Crossroads," June 7-9, 1977.
7. Giorgio Galli is a vigorous exponent of this position. See his book, *Storia della Democrazia Cristiana* and his chapter in *Dall '68 a oggi, come siamo e come eravamo.*
8. Giulio C. Lepschy, "The Language of Mussolini," *The Journal of Italian History*, Winter 1978, p. 531.
9. Gabriele Calvi, "La frattura tra valori e scelte politiche in Italia," *Rivista italiana di scienza politica*, April 1980, pp. 125-47.
10. Giorgio Napolitano, *Intervista sul PCI*, ed. Eric J. Hobsbawn (Bari: Laterza, 1976), pp. 72-73.
11. Giorgio Amendola, "Ipotesi sulla riunificazione," *Rinascita*, November 28, 1964, pp. 8-9.
12. Norman Kogan, Carlo Mongardini, Mario P. Salani, and Maurizio Maravalle, *Realtà e immagine della politica estera italiana* (Milan: Giuffrè, 1980).
13. *Public Opinion*, July/August 1978, p. 21.

BIBLIOGRAPHY

Acquaviva, Sabino S. *Guerriglia e guerra rivoluzionaria in Italia.* Milan: Rizzoli, 1978.

Alberoni, Francesco. *Italia in transformazione.* Bologna: Il Mulino, 1976.

Allum, P. A. *Italy—Republic Without Government?* New York: Norton, 1973.

———. *Politics and Society in Post-War Naples.* Cambridge: Cambridge University Press, 1973.

Ammassari, Gloria Pirzio. *La politica della Confindustria.* Naples: Liguori, 1976.

Andreatta, Nino. *Una economia bloccata, 1969-1973.* Bologna: Il Mulino, 1973.

Barnes, Samuel H. *Party Democracy: Politics in an Italian Socialist Federation.* New Haven: Yale University Press, 1967.

———. *Representation in Italy: Institutionalized Tradition and Electoral Choice.* Chicago: University of Chicago Press, 1977.

Belloni, Frank P., and Dennis C. Beller, editors. *Faction Politics: Political Parties and Factionalism in Comparative Perspective.* Santa Barbara: ABC-Clio Press, 1978.

Berlinguer, Enrico. *La questione comunista.* Rome: Riuniti, 1975.

Blackmer, Donald L. M. *Unity in Diversity, Italian Communism and the Communist World.* Cambridge, Mass.: MIT Press, 1968.

Blackmer, Donald L. M., and Sidney Tarrow, editors. *Communism in Italy and France.* Princeton: Princeton University Press, 1975.

Blackmer, Donald L. M., and Annie Kriegel. *The International Role of the Communist Parties of Italy and France.* Cambridge, Mass.: Center for International Affairs, Harvard University, 1975.

Caciagli, Mario, and Alberto Spreafico, editors. *Un sistema politico alla prova.* Bologna: Il Mulino, 1975.

Carli, Guido. *Intervista sul capitalismo italiano.* Bari: Laterza, 1977.

Castronovo, Valerio, editor. *L'Italia contemporanea 1945-1975.* Turin: Einaudi, 1976.

Clark, Burton R. *Academic Power in Italy: Bureaucracy and Oligarchy in a National University System.* Chicago: University of Chicago Press, 1977.

Contini, B. *Lo sviluppo di una economia parallela.* Milan: Comunità, 1979.

Dal '68 a oggi, Come siamo e come eravamo. Bari: Laterza, 1979.

D'Angelo, Massimo, Giuseppe Sacco, and Gian Andrea Sandri. *La cooperazione industriale tra Italia e paesi in via di sviluppo.* Bologna: Il Mulino, 1979.

D'Antonio, Mariano. *Sviluppo e crisi del capitalismo italiano 1950-1972.* Bari: De Donato, 1973.

Di Palma, Giuseppe. *Political Syncretism in Italy: Historical Coalition Strategies and the Present Crisis.* Berkeley: Institute of International Studies, University of California, 1978.

———. *Surviving Without Governing: The Italian Parties in Parliament.* Berkeley: University of California Press, 1976.

Di Renzo, Gordon J. *Personality, Power and Politics.* Notre Dame: University of Notre Dame Press, 1967.

Dogan, Mattei, and Orazio M. Petracca. *Partiti politici e strutture sociali in Italia.* Milan: Comunità, 1968.

Evans, Robert H. *A Venetian Community, an Italian Village.* Notre Dame: University of Notre Dame Press, 1976.

Farneti, Paolo, editor. *Il sistema politico italiano.* Bologna: Il Mulino, 1973.

Filo della Torre, Paolo, Edward Mortimer, and Jonathan Story, editors. *Eurocommunism: Myth or Reality?* Harmondsworth: Penguin Books, 1979.

Forte, Francesco. *La strategie delle riforme.* Milan: Etas Kompass, 1968.

Franco, Giampiero, editor. *Sviluppo e crisi dell'economia italiana.* Milan: Etas Libri, 1979.

Fried, Robert C. *Planning the Eternal City.* New Haven: Yale University Press, 1973.

Fua, Giorgio. *Occupazione e capacità produttive: La realtà italiana.* Bologna: Il Mulino, 1976.

Galli, Giorgio. *Il bipartitismo imperfetto.* Bologna: Il Mulino, 1966.

———. *Storia della Democrazia Cristiana.* Bari: Laterza, 1978.

Galli, Giorgio, and Alfonso Prandi. *Patterns of Political Participation in Italy.* New Haven: Yale University Press, 1970.

Gorresio, Vittorio. *Berlinguer.* Milan: Feltrinelli, 1976.

Graziano, Luigi, and Sidney Tarrow, editors. *La crisi italiana.* 2 vols. Turin: Einaudi, 1979.

Grindrod, Muriel. *Italy.* New York: Praeger, 1968.

Istituto Affari Internazionali. *L'Italia nella politica internazionale.* 7 vols. Milan: Comunità, 1974-1980.

Italy, Presidency of the Council of Ministers. *The State Participation System in Italy.* Rome: Istituto Poligrafico dello Stato, 1977.

Keefe, Eugene K., editor. *Area Handbook for Italy.* Washington: Government Printing Office, 1977.

Kogan, Norman, Carlo Mongardini, Mario P. Salani, and Maurizio Maravalle. *Realtà e immagine della politica estera italiana.* Milan: Giuffrè, 1980.

LaPalombara, Joseph. *Italy: The Politics of Planning.* National Planning Series, No. 7. Syracuse: Syracuse University Press, 1966.

LaPalombara, Joseph, and Stephen Blank. *Multinational Corporations and National Elites: A Study in Tensions.* New York: The Conference Board, 1976.

Levi, Arrigo. *Un'idea dell'Italia.* Milan: Mondadori, 1979.

L'Italia negli ultimi trent'anni, Rassegna critica degli studi. Bologna: Il Mulino, 1978.

Low-Beer, John R. *Protest and Participation: The New Working Class in Italy.* Cambridge: Cambridge University Press, 1978.

Magister, Sandro. *La politica vaticana e l'Italia, 1943-1978.* Rome: Riuniti, 1979.

Mammarella, Giuseppe. *Il partito comunista italiano 1945-1975.* Florence: Vallecchi, 1976.

——. *L'Italia dalla caduta del fascismo ad oggi.* Bologna: Il Mulino, 1978.

Napolitano, Giorgio. *Intervista sul PCI.* Edited by Eric J. Hobsbawm. Bari: Laterza, 1976.

Negri, Antonio. *Il dominio e il sabottagio: Sul metodo marxista della trasformazione sociale.* Milan: Feltrinelli, 1977.

Nichols, Peter. *Italia, Italia.* London: Macmillan, 1973.

——. *The Politics of the Vatican.* New York: Praeger, 1968.

Parisi, Arturo, and Gianfranco Pasquino, editors. *Continuità e mutamento elettorale in Italia.* Bologna: Il Mulino, 1977.

Pedrazzi, Luigi. *La politica scolastica del centro-sinistra.* Bologna: Il Mulino, 1972.

Peggio, Eugenio. *La crisi economica italiana.* Milan: Rizzoli, 1976.

Penniman, Howard R., editor. *Italy at the Polls: The Parliamentary Elections of 1976.* Washington: American Enterprise Institute for Public Policy Research, 1977.

Posner, M. W., and S. J. Woolf. *Italian Public Enterprise.* Cambridge, Mass.: Harvard University Press, 1967.

Putnam, Robert D. *The Beliefs of Politicians, Ideology, Conflict, and Democracy in Britain and Italy.* New Haven: Yale University Press, 1973.

Ranney, Austin, and Giovanni Sartori, editors. *Eurocommunism: The Italian Case.* Washington: American Enterprise Institute for Public Policy Research, 1978.

Ronchey, Alberto. *Accade in Italia, 1968-1977.* Milan: Rizzoli, 1977.

Salvati, Michele. *Il sistema economico italiano: analisi di una crisi.* Bologna: Il Mulino, 1975.

Sartori, Giovanni, editor. *Correnti, frazionalismo e fazioni nei partiti italiani.* Bologna: Il Mulino, 1973.

Scandaletti, Paolo. *La fine del compromesso.* Venice: Marsilio, 1979.

Silj, Alessandro. *Never Again Without a Rifle: The Origins of Italian Terrorism.* New York: Karz, 1979.

Statera, Gianni. *Death of a Utopia.* New York: Oxford University Press, 1975.

Sylos Labini, Paolo. *Saggio sulle classi sociali.* Bari: Laterza, 1974.

Tamburrano, Giuseppe. *Storia e cronaca del centro-sinistra.* Milan: Feltrinelli, 1971.

Tannenbaum, Edward R., and Emiliana P. Noether, editors. *Modern Italy, A Topical History Since 1861.* New York: New York University Press, 1974.

Teodori, Massimo, editor. *Per l'alternativa.* Milan: Feltrinelli, 1975.

——. *The New Left: A Documentary History.* Indianapolis: Bobbs-Merrill, 1969.

Tökés, Rudolf L., editor. *Eurocommunism and Détente.* New York: New York University Press, 1978.

Trent'anni della CGIL (1944-1974). Rome: Sindacale Italiana, 1975.

Vannicelli, Primo. *Italy, NATO and the European Community.* Cambridge, Mass.: Center for International Affairs, Harvard University, 1974.

Vettori, G. *La sinistra extraparlamentare in Italia.* Rome: Newton Compton Italiana, 1973.

Willis, F. Roy. *Italy Chooses Europe.* New York: Oxford University Press, 1971.

Wiskemann, Elizabeth. *Italy Since 1945.* New York: St. Martin's Press, 1971.

Zagari, Mario. *Superare le sfide.* Milan: Rizzoli, 1976.

Zariski, Raphael. *Italy: The Politics of Uneven Development.* Hinsdale, Ill.: Dryden, 1972.

Zuckerman, Alan S. *The Politics of Faction: Christian Democratic Rule in Italy.* New Haven: Yale University Press, 1979.

INDEX

ABOUT THE AUTHOR

NORMAN KOGAN is Professor of Political Science at The University of Connecticut, Storrs. He has also been a Fulbright research professor and Fulbright senior lecturer at the University of Rome, Italy. From 1967 to 1976 he was executive secretary-treasurer of the Society for Italian Historical Studies. From 1975 to 1977 he was president of the Conference Group on Italian Politics. He is a member of the Board of Editors of *Comparative Politics* and of the Board of Directors of the America-Italy Society. In 1971 he was made a Knight in the Order of Merit of the Italian Republic by the president of the Republic.

Professor Kogan has published in the fields of political science and history. His books include: *Italy and the Allies* (Cambridge, Mass.: Harvard University Press, 1956); *The Government of Italy* (New York: Crowell, 1962); *The Politics of Italian Foreign Policy* (New York: Praeger, 1963); *A Political History of Postwar Italy*, Vol. I (New York: Praeger, 1966). In addition he has published chapters in edited volumes. His articles have appeared in *The Western Political Quarterly*, *The Journal of Politics*, *Comparative Politics*, *International Journal*, *Polity*, *Studies in Comparative Communism*, *European Review*, *Italian Quarterly*, *The Yale Law Journal*, *Indiana Law Journal*, *Il Ponte*, *Il Mondo*, and *Il Movimento di Liberazione in Italia*.

Professor Kogan holds a B.A. and a Ph.D. from the University of Chicago.